On Music, Sense, Affect and Voice

READING AUGUSTINE

Series editor:

Miles Hollingworth

Reading Augustine offers personal and close readings of St. Augustine of Hippo from leading philosophers and religious scholars. Its aim is to make clear Augustine's importance to contemporary thought and to present Augustine not only or primarily as a pre-eminent Christian thinker but as a philosophical, spiritual, literary and intellectual icon of the West.

Volumes in the series:

On Ethics, Politics and Psychology in the Twenty-First Century, John Rist

On Love, Confession, Surrender and the Moral Self, Ian Clausen

On Education, Formation, Citizenship and the Lost Purpose of Learning, Joseph Clair

On Creativity, Liberty, Love and the Beauty of the Law, Todd Breyfogle

On Consumer Culture, Identity, The Church and the Rhetorics of Delight (forthcoming), Mark Clavier

On Self-Harm, Narcissism, Atonement and the Vulnerable Christ (forthcoming), David Vincent Meconi

On God, The Soul, Evil and the Rise of Christianity (forthcoming), John Peter Kenney

On Music, Sense, Affect and Voice (forthcoming), Carol Harrison

On Music, Sense, Affect and Voice

Carol Harrison

t&tclark

LONDON • NEW YORK • OXFORD • NEW DELHI • SYDNEY

T&T CLARK
Bloomsbury Publishing Plc
50 Bedford Square, London, WC1B 3DP, UK
1385 Broadway, New York, NY 10018, USA

BLOOMSBURY, T&T CLARK and the T&T Clark logo are
trademarks of Bloomsbury Publishing Plc

First published in Great Britain 2019

Cover design: Terry Woodley
Series design by Catherine Wood
Cover image: Carol Harrison

A catalogue record for this book is available from the British Library.

Library of Congress Cataloging-in-Publication Data
Names: Klemme, Heiner, editor. | Kuehn, Manfred, editor. Title: The Bloomsbury dictionary of
eighteenth-century German philosophers | edited by Heiner F. Klemme and Manfred Kuehn.
Other titles: Dictionary of eighteenth-century German philosophers Description: New York:
Bloomsbury Publishing Plc, 2016. | Originally published under title: Dictionary of eighteenth-
century German philosophers: London: Continuum, 2010. | Includes bibliographical
references and index. Identifiers: LCCN 2015040044| ISBN 9781474255974 (pb) |
ISBN 9781474256001 (epub) | ISBN 9781474255981 (epdf)
Subjects: LCSH: Philosophers–Germany–Dictionaries. | Philosophy, German–18th century–
Dictionaries. Classification: LCC B2615.D53 2016 | DDC 193–dc23 LC record available at
http://lccn.loc.gov/2015040044

ISBN: HB: 978-1-5013-2625-7
     PB: 978-1-5013-2626-4
    ePDF: 978-1-5013-2628-8
   eBook: 978-1-5013-2627-1

Series: Library of New Testament Studies, 2345678X, volume 286

Typeset by Integra Software Services Pvt. Ltd.
Printed and bound in Great Britain

To find out more about our authors and books visit www.bloomsbury.com
and sign up for our newsletters.

CONTENTS

ACKNOWLEDGEMENTS

This book would not have been written without the research leave I was granted by the Faculty of Theology and Religion, Oxford University, and Christ Church Cathedral, Oxford. During this leave I held a British Academy Senior Research Fellowship at the British School at Rome and worked for a semester as Augustine Fellow at the Augustinian Institute, Villanova. For these opportunities to undertake uninterrupted research and for conversations with colleagues and friends in both places, I am deeply grateful. I would also like to thank Miles Hollingworth, without whom this book would never have happened; for his enthusiastic support and encouragment at every stage of its progress. For help in the final stages I am indebted to my research student, Jenny Rallens, for her expert advice on Latin.

This book brings together two of my great passions, Augustine and music, with thanks to all those who have shared and inspired these passions over the years: my colleagues and students in Durham and Oxford; my son, Isaac; Christ Church Cathedral choir. It is dedicated to Stephen Darlington, Organist and Director of Music at Christ Church, on his retirement.

Introduction

Augustine offers us a definition of music at the beginning of his very early treatise *On Music* (*De musica*): music is the knowledge of measuring well; *musica est scientia bene modulandi*.[1] It is almost impossible to translate this deceptively simple definition, and having framed it, Augustine and his pupil (the work takes the form of a dialogue) struggle to unpack each of the key terms.

They begin with *modulandi* (from *modus* (measure)): 'Music is the knowledge of measuring well.'[2] But what is being measured? We will see in our first chapter that in the classical and late antique period music was inseparably associated with poetry, with words which could be rhythmically tapped or beaten out. The theoretical structure of rhythm was taught and analysed through the various types of poetic metre which, for centuries, had been handed down by the grammarians and poets. In this context music was a way of structuring the sound of the spoken voice so that it communicated, not only through words but through a rhythmic beat. The measure which defines music is therefore first of all a form of rhythmic sound which can be performed or beaten out.

Measure also refers to movement: a sound or beat is only well measured or rhythmic because it is performed, and that performance is one in which sound moves through time, structuring time, and as it were, measuring it out. For Augustine and his pupil measure is therefore found, not only in poetry but also in dance, where the body moves rhythmically to a measured beat.

---

[1] *mus.* 1.2.2.
[2] This is often translated 'Music is the knowledge of modulating well' but I don't think that the English word 'modulation' quite captures the meaning.

What is being measured in music is therefore movement: the movement of sound, of the voice and of the body. Such movement comprehends singing, playing an instrument, the voice of the nightingale, as well as the gestures of an actor or dancer on the stage.

But Augustine's definition doesn't stop there: *musica est scientia bene modulandi*; music is the knowledge (*scientia*) of measuring well (*bene*). To measure well (*bene*) is, of course, inherent in the idea of rhythmic movement; if it was not well measured it would not be rhythmic but disordered, random, dissonant and disfigured. So *bene* – to measure *well* – has aesthetic connotations: it implies that whatever is measured is measured appropriately, fittingly, and with 'good' measure, as it were. It also has ontological, ethical and theological overtones, for Augustine teaches that music, as measured movement, is written into the nature of created reality; it is the order which must be observed in virtuous action; it inspires a love of God, a love which restores dissonant and disfigured movement. But this is to run ahead.

Scientia is perhaps the most revealing term: it is sometimes translated 'science'; music is the science or knowledge (*scientia*) of measuring well. This begs the question of *how* we know what good measure is. Is it a matter for the reason, mind and intellect, or is it a matter of sense, memory, imitation and practice? Augustine and his pupil are well aware that it is both: it is both a matter of theory and of practice; it is manifest in the theoretical knowledge of the grammarian and in the voice of the poet.

In the chapters that follow we will see that the question of how we know is a fundamental one for Augustine. As an intellectual, a scholar and a teacher, trained in the disciplines of the liberal arts, he wants to hold fast to the rational, intellectual theory of music, or measured movement, as it exists independently of sensuous, temporal performance. But as a Christian convert, deeply aware of his fallen inability to apprehend truth and acutely sensitive to the compelling and moving power of the Church's Psalms, hymns and songs, he found himself involuntarily overwhelmed by precisely that sensuous, temporal performance he was so suspicious of. It is in this context that we will consider what I have called the 'conversion of the senses' in Chapter 1, where I focus on his early treatise *On Music*.

Of course, Augustine's ambivalence does not disappear, but we will see that however much he insists on the rational and intellectual, it is more often than not his experience of the affective and emotive power of music that brings about a 'knowing' that is no longer simply a matter of knowledge (*scientia*) but also of what he calls 'loving devotion' (*affectus pietatis*).[3] When we take account of the fact that the source of all measured movement is God, then its power to inspire such devotion naturally follows. It is in this sense that we will speak of a conversion of the affections, in Chapter 2, where we examine Augustine's encounter with music in Milan – and especially Ambrose's hymns – around the time of his conversion.

As Augustine witnesses, music in a very real sense democratized the Church: it conveyed the truths of the faith to all, regardless of age, gender, education or social standing. In the final chapter, on 'the conversion of the voice' I argue that this was as much a matter of sound (*uox*) as of words alone. We will see that the measured movement of Augustine's earlier definition of music sometimes gives way to the much wilder sound of what he calls 'jubilation' – the wordless cry or shout of joy which spontaneously erupts from the singing of the Psalms. He likens it to the singing of peasants in the fields, rather than to classical verse, and observes that it expresses what words cannot express. We can appreciate how much Augustine's understanding of music was transformed in this Christian context when he maintains that the ability to sing with jubilation is a technique for singing (*modum cantandi*)[4] which God teaches even those who have no knowledge of the theory of music, so that they can praise His otherwise unknowable and ineffable greatness. Music thus became, for Augustine, the voice of the heart, sounded in songs of praise, which joins the singing of the Church to that of the eternal song of the angels in the courts of heaven.

---

[3] *conf.* 9.6.14; 10.33.50.
[4] *en.Ps.* 99.4.

1

The Conversion of the Senses

God, creator of all things
And ruler of the heavens, fitting
The day with beauteous light
And the night with the grace of sleep

Deus creator omnium
Polique rector, uestiens
Diem decoro lumine,
Noctem soporis gratia

(Ambrose *Deus Creator Omnium* (Ramsay
(1997) 170–171))

How sweet the moonlight sleeps upon this bank!
Here will we sit and let the sounds of music
Creep in our ears: soft stillness and the night
Become the touches of sweet harmony.
Sit, Jessica. Look how the floor of heaven
Is thick inlaid with patines of bright gold:
There's not the smallest orb which thou behold'st
But in his motion like an angel sings,
Still quiring to the young-eyed cherubins;
Such harmony is in immortal souls;
But whilst this muddy vesture of decay
Doth grossly close it in, we cannot hear it.

(Shakespeare *Merchant of Venice* Act 5, scene 1)

When early Christian theologians turned to address the subject of music it was, at once, immediately obvious and yet rather disconcerting. This was first and foremost due to the fact that music was thought about and practised in two very different contexts, by two rather different groups of people: for the educated minority it was a rational, academic discipline, concerned with the mathematical laws of rhythm and harmony – one of the seven liberal arts (*artes liberales*),[1] which it was the privilege of free citizens to study and which formed their shared culture; for the uneducated majority it was something that resonated and reverberated in their ears through the sounds of instrumental and vocal performance. Music was therefore both a theory and a practice; the disconcerting thing was the question of how, or even if, theory and practice were related.[2]

The answer is not the straightforward one which we moderns are readily able to rehearse: that music theory provides the universally acknowledged rules for all (or at least most) types of musical composition and practice. The ancients did not see the relation between music as a liberal discipline and music in performance in anything like the same way: one was a matter of eternal, immutable, incorporeal truths to be understood by the intellect; the other was a matter of temporal, mutable, all too sensuous sound – worse, it was often practised by dubious characters in dodgy contexts and played on the most distracting of human passions.[3] Was there any useful or

---

[1]Grammar, rhetoric, dialectic, arithmetic, music, geometry and astronomy (or philosophy). On the liberal arts and the role they played in Augustine's thought, see Hadot (1984); Harrison (2006) 41–48; Marrou (1958) 187–235, and more generally, Kaster (1988). On music theory in late antiquity, see Matheisen (1999) 497–608. Possible influences on Augustine's thought on music include Aristides Quintilianus *De Musica*; Plutarch *De Musica*; Aristoxenus; the Pythagoreans, Nichomachus of Gerasa, Ptolemy, Theo of Smyra, who he may have encountered in translation or synopsis. For more detail on these sources, see Jeserich (2013) 97–100.

[2]McKinnon's (2000) 779 observations are representative: '*musica*.... had little to do with the modern notion of what constitutes music, it would be a mistake even to identify it with the contemporary subject of music theory.... it had nothing to do with the everyday music of its time and concentrated instead on the construction of abstract tonal systems (scales) which utilized the full repository of ancient mathematical learning'.

[3]Performers do not receive a good press in classical literature. Aristotle, for example, advises against education in playing or performance

for the performer does not take part in it for his own improvement but for his hearers' pleasure, and that a vulgar pleasure, owing to which we do not

acceptable link to be made, then, between these two manifestations of music, or were they simply entirely alien entities which happened to share the same name?

Henri Irenée Marrou,[4] one of the few scholars to have devoted much attention to Augustine on the subject music, is representative of a scholarly approach to the subject of music in antiquity which entirely divorces theory and practice. He argues, for example, that the word *musica* was only ever used by Augustine of the liberal art, while words such as the verb *cantare* and related words such as *cantus, canticum, cantilena* were used of performed music.[5] The latter, he observes, was 'foreign to the culture of the upper class' and was generally regarded as the activity of 'despised professions'.[6] The liberal art of *musica* was something 'reserved for the elite and denied to the masses'.[7] Whereas we value a sensibility to performed music, Marrou observes that this was alien to classical culture: that a classical philosopher, such as Augustine, immersed in the Platonic tradition, would have possessed no notion of such sensibility – or indeed, of 'art' as we would now understand it; rather, he comments, 'He was simply aware of *sensus*, sensation, which is much less honourable; it is the least elevated activity of the soul, where the demands of the body play a detrimental role.'[8] In this book we

---

consider performing to be proper for free men, but somewhat menial; and indeed performers do become vulgar, since the object at which they aim is a low one, as vulgarity in the audience usually influences the music' *Politics* 8.7 (Loeb 264. 667–669)
Clearly, his comments depend on context (here, musical competitions). He has much to say that is positive about performance in other contexts, both for the player and the hearer.
[4]Marrou (1958) 197–204. He writes: 'Ce serait un contre sens très grave que de traduire *musica* par notre "musique".... pour Augustin, la *musica* est une science mathématique au même titre que l'arithmétique ou la géometrie (197) ... Il n'est pas possible d'être plus clair: la *musica* n'est pas notre art, c'est une *scientia*, un faisceau organizé de connaissances rationnelles' (200) ... Dans la mesure où elle aspire à entrer dans une culture philosophique, la *musica* doit se dépouiller de tout ce qui fait pour nous son essence, de tout son caractère "artistique"; elle doit se ramener à sa proper théorie (201)'.
[5]Marrou (1958) 197 n. 4.
[6]Marrou (1958) 202 '.... cet art est toujours restée en principe étrangère à la culture normale des hautes classes.... aux professions les plus avilies'.
[7]Marrou (1958) 202 'Elle est réservée à l'élite, refusée à la masse'.
[8]Ibid. 203.

will be arguing that in his reflections on music Augustine, in fact, subverts what Marrou depicts as an elite culture which had no place for the actual performance of music; that, in practice, he possessed an acute sensibility to music, which, although it caused him some ambivalence, he did not ultimately deny or avoid. Rather, we will demonstrate that he was increasingly persuaded that it was only by means of temporal, mutable, sensuous sound, rather than eternal, immutable, rational rules, that the truth which the philosophers sought could be apprehended by fallen human beings. We will see that he maintained that this truth was known by faith rather than reason; by love rather than the intellect; by the masses rather than the elite. In other words, we will argue that for Augustine the apprehension of truth was less a rational exercise and more a matter of what we might call, following the poet Geoffrey Hill, 'sensuous intelligence', and that in this, music had a key role to play.

In the same Platonic vein, writing under the pseudonym he used as a music critic – Henri Davenson – Marrou further argues that, even when sounded music delights us, it does so because it evokes an ideal sound or archetype within – one which we hear with our inner ear, in the silence of the soul – and that it is only according to this archetype that we are able to hear and to judge performed music.[9] In relation to musical composition he therefore observes that 'the composer imitates the silent music which he discovers in the abstraction of his heart in sonorous forms';[10] that 'composition is imitation ... of a spiritual harmony, perceived in the silence of the soul by an inner ear'.[11]

In this instance, Marrou's distinction between an inner and an outer music, heard by the inward or outward ear, by the mind or the senses respectively, does, in fact, resonate with what Augustine sometimes observes – at least in theory: he distinguishes between what he calls a 'verse in the mind' – in other words the eternal and immutable laws or rules which govern verse and which allow us to judge it – and a 'verse in the voice', in other words poetry or music performed and heard, which is but an imitation of the inward

---

[9]Davenson (1942) 23–48.
[10]Davenson (1942) 47 'le compositeur imite avec des forms sonores la musique silencieuse qu'il découvre dans l'abstrait de son coeur'.
[11]Ibid. 48 'la composition est l'imitation.... d'une harmonie spirituelle, perçue dans le silence de l'âme par une oreille intérieure'.

laws.[12] Commenting on 'the age of this age' in contrast to 'this age' (Psalm 9.6) he observes,

> The age of this age is that which consists in unchangeable eternity. It is like a verse which exists in the mind and a verse which is spoken (*uersus in animo, et uersus in uoce*). The former is understood, the latter is heard; the former regulates the latter. That is why the former is effective in art and endures, whereas the latter sounds in the air and is gone. Likewise, the mode of being of this changeable world is defined by that unchangeable world, which is spoken of as the age of this age. And for this reason the latter endures in the art (*in arte Dei*), that is, in the wisdom and power of God, but the other is carried on through the providential administration of the created order (*in creaturae administratione peragitur*).[13]

What we will need to ask, in what follows, is whether this 'art' – here understood as the inward, eternal, immutable archetype of verse, in a Platonic context; the wisdom and power of God, in a Christian context, – is indeed something we are now able, in practice, to comprehend and use in order to judge. I will argue that in a theological context – where he finds himself taking account of creation from nothing, the Fall and God's providential economy – Augustine tends to speak, not in terms of the Platonic distinction between eternal, ideal form and temporal imitation but rather in terms of our perception of the 'art', or wisdom and power of God, by the senses: that the 'verse in the mind' is only perceived *through* the 'verse in the voice'; that the 'invisible things of God are known through the things that are made' (Rom 1.20); and that the art and wisdom of God is incarnated and revealed to us in the Son made flesh. In other words, I will argue that Augustine teaches that the art, wisdom and power of God are only perceived through what he calls, in the text we have just cited, 'the providential administration of the created order', and most especially, through what he will

---

[12]Cf. *uera rel.* 42 – where Augustine distinguishes between the art of poetry, that is, the eternal, unchanging rules of verse, and poetry itself, and observes that the transient, successive syllables of a verse are 'beautiful as exhibiting the faint traces of the beauty which the art of poetry keeps steadfastly and unchangeably'.

[13]*en.Ps.* 9.7.

identify in book 6 of *De musica*, as the temporal, sensuous music of God's creating, ordering and redeeming love, which, by inspiring our love, returns us to its source and end.[14]

The art of music

Augustine was the only early Christian writer to devote a work specifically to music – his *De musica*.[15] He tells us that he began to write it after his baptism (Easter 387) and after having returned from Italy to his home town of Thagaste in North Africa (388/9).[16] He probably completed it towards the end of 391. Living in a lay community of 'servants of God', free of his demanding job as municipal rhetor, having relinquished any plans to marry, and well before priestly or episcopal duties took their toll, he presumably did so with a liberating sense of having the time and space to undertake ambitious projects. It is one of the few surviving works we now possess of what he tells us was a projected series of seven, devoted to each of the seven liberal arts, which he began to write in Milan and which he hoped would enable him to continue his journey from, as he puts it, 'the corporeal to the incorporeal' (*retr.* 1.6).[17] In other words, it appears that by following a rigorous programme of study, he intended to train his mind, and those of his companions, through intellectual and moral purification, to dwell on eternal and immutable truths rather than the messy stuff of everyday business.

---

[14]*mus.* 6.4.7.

[15]For the text of *De musica*, I have used CSEL 102 (ed. Jacobsson). For books 1–5, I have used the translation by Robert Catesby Taliaferro which appears in *The Fathers of the Church* 4 (1947) 153–384 (with some revisions). For book 6, I have used the edition, translation and commentary by Jacobsson (2002).

Bibliothèque Augustinienne 7 (1947) Latin text with French translation and notes by Guy Finaert and F.J. Thonnard; Hentschel (2002) Latin text with German translation are also very useful.

[16]*retr.* 1.6 It is not clear how much of the work was written in Milan and how much on his return to Africa. He writes: 'But I wrote those same six books [of *De musica*] after having been baptized and after having returned to Africa from Italy, since I had barely started on that discipline while I was in Milan' (*Sed eosdem sex libros jam baptizatus, jamque ex Italia regressus In Africam scripsi, incohaueram quippe tantummodo istam apud Mediolanum disciplinam*).

[17]*retr.* 1.6.

Returning to Milan in 387, fresh from a post-conversion, classical-type retreat in the country villa of a friend, which had been devoted to philosophical dialogue on the big questions, he wrote the book on grammar and began others on dialectic, rhetoric, geometry, arithmetic and philosophy.[18] It is clear that Augustine the new convert had not left the schoolroom entirely behind, but evidently intended to take it with him, insofar as it proved useful in coming to terms with his newly embraced faith.

Augustine's *De musica* is thus a distinctly odd work – at least for us: a school book *On Music* as a liberal discipline, a dialogue in which the master works with evident accomplishment and skill to lead his pupil through the technicalities, definitions and practice of poetic metre, to cover the 'curriculum', as it were. What was Augustine, the new Christian convert, thinking of and what can we learn about a Christian appreciation of music – as a theoretical discipline as well as in practice – from this treatise?

I don't think anyone in the ancient world would have lifted an eyebrow on first encountering the *De musica*; at least, their eyebrows would no doubt have remained comfortably in place over the course of its first five books and then shot up when they reached the sixth book, which does proceed to go rather unsettlingly off track from what had no doubt so far struck them as a pretty standard treatise on the rhythmical aspect of the liberal discipline, or art, of music – much like all the others they had been forced to read at school.[19]

For the first five books of this work, which we will consider in detail below, consist of a careful analysis of poetic rhythm or metre, and although this might seem odd to his modern readers, it would have been precisely what his contemporaries expected. Indeed, if there is anything which might be identified as bridging the two types of music we have just encountered – the liberal art of music and performed music; the verse in the mind and the verse in the voice – it is poetry, which was generally understood to be synonymous with music. As Thomas Habinek observes, the basic distinction in the ancient world in this context is not one between

---

[18]*retr.* 1.6 Augustine tells us that he has already lost these works. *De dialectica* (ed. Pinborg and Jackson (1975)) survives.

[19]Taliaferro (FC 4: 160–161) suggests that even book 6 is a recognizable genre: 'The last book deals with music in its cosmological and theological aspects, corresponding to the last book of Aristides [Quintilianus] and the well-known tradition of the Timaeus.... All this is perfectly obvious and perfectly usual.'

poetry and song (or music) but between what he calls everyday speech and 'ritualised' speech: 'speech made special through metre, diction, accompanying bodily movement or performance in a ritual context'. He notes that the Latin language describes such ritualized speech 'with verbs based on the root *can* – such as *cano* and *canto*, and the related noun *carmen*'.[20] In this sense, the definition of song is not so much a matter of genre as of those features which mark it out, or ritualise it, in contrast to everyday speech. Thus, for users of Latin, there was no fundamental distinction between poetry and other types of song, such as chant, hymns, incantations, recitation or even dancing; rather the distinction was, as Habinek puts it, 'between song and speech via the use of the expressions *cano/ carmen* and *loquor/locuta*'.[21]

Classical and Christian treatises 'On music' – at least, those on its rhythmical aspect[22] – therefore turn out, on closer inspection, to be (somewhat disappointingly for the theologian) treatises on poetic metre. Anyone familiar with classical poetry will be aware that it is, indeed, fundamentally a matter of rhythmic, quantitative or accented verse, which was learned and practised in a highly technical, challengingly mathematical and rational manner. Thus, poetry, which could undeniably express the heights and depths of human emotion and imagination, was always and everywhere formally structured and analysable according to a (for the outsider) fiendishly complicated set of conventions, which were universally recognized and adopted as a matter of tradition and authority. The poet was, in effect, performing an extraordinarily skilful balancing act between intellectual theory and voiced expression and it is this combination of theory and practice which opens up, for our purposes, a context in which the rational discipline or liberal art of

---

[20]Habinek (2005) 1.
[21]Habinek (2005) 79. Though he also points out that Ennius and Horace are notable exceptions to this rule.
[22]The other aspect of music that was commonly treated in classical works was melody though, sadly, Augustine never got round to his projected work on this subject: 'I wrote six books exclusively on rhythm, and I was, I admit, planning to write perhaps another six on melody (*de melo*), when I hoped that I would have the leisure. But after the burden of cares about the Church was imposed on me, all those trifles fled from my hands so that I can now scarcely find the manuscript' (*ep.* 101.3). For a glimpse of Augustine's understanding of harmony, see *trin.* 4.1–2; *en.Ps.* 150.7.

music and what we might call the sensuous performance of music might be thought of within the same frame.

First, we might well ask why the identification of song and poetry was so obvious to the ancients; why was the same word used synonymously of both verse and singing? We no longer possess any real sense of what the singing sounded like,[23] whereas we do have a very clear sense of what the poetry was meant to sound like from the many ancient treatises, like Augustine's *De musica*, which deal with the rules for quantitative poetic metre or, in the Greek world, with the markings which indicate pitch or accent/stress. The fact that the same word was used to refer to music and poetry, song and verse, singing and reciting, and that we know so much about the latter, means that we can reasonably deduce a great deal about ancient perceptions of the former, which otherwise remains inaccessible and unheard. If poetry is also music, then music must have also been poetry; in other words, the music must have been primarily a matter of rhythm and, in some contexts, pitch. Both poetry and music, then, were a distinctive expression of the eternal and immutable art of number in the form of ordered sound – in Habineck's terms, a form of ritualized speech.

It is certainly in this way that Augustine presents the relationship between performed music and the liberal art of music – in other words, between sound and what it signifies – in his *De ordine*, a work on divine providence, written just before his *De musica*. In this work, composed while on retreat immediately after his conversion in 386, he traces an ascent by reason through the liberal arts. It is an ascent which is based on the conviction that all the liberal arts are rational and that a study of them will therefore allow the student to move from temporal, mutable traces of reason to immutable and eternal reason – a process he sums up as a movement from the 'corporeal to the incorporeal'.[24] The first three liberal arts – grammar, dialectic and rhetoric – are, he observes, reasonable (*rationabile*) in the sense that they use 'discourse ... to teach correctly'. The remaining four are reasonable in the sense that they afford 'pleasure

---

[23]Though there have been attempts to imaginatively reconstruct it, e.g. Marcel Pérès and Ensemble Organum *Chants de l'Église Milanaise* and *Chants de l'Église de Rome*, Harmonia Mundi.
[24]Cf *mus*.6.2.2 *a corporeis ad incorporea*; *Retr.* 1.6. *per corporalia cupiens ad incorporalia*; Du Roy (1966) 284; Solignac (1958) 120–124; Svoboda (1933) 29–34 for sources, notably Varro.

[by which we] find delight in contemplation'.[25] Turning to music as the fourth stage in his ascent, Augustine therefore turns from reason in *discourse* (*in dicendo*) to reason in *pleasure* (*in delectando*).[26] The movement from reason in discourse to reason apprehended in pleasure is a significant turning point and leads him to consider just what it is that makes musical sound pleasing; how it communicates something to us so that we do not simply hear it with the ears but also delight in contemplation of it.[27] The short answer is that, like other arts which are seen or heard, and which afford pleasure to the viewer or hearer, it is reason itself, manifest in the rhythm – what Augustine calls the number (*numerus* = rhythm) – of music, which both constitutes music and makes it something delightful and pleasing. Thus, he comments,

> Insofar as we have been able to investigate, we now detect certain traces of reason (*uestigia rationis*) in the senses, and with regard to sight and hearing, we find it in pleasure itself .... With regard to the ears, when we say that a harmony (*concentum*) is reasonable and that a rhythmic poem is reasonably composed (*cantumque numerosum rationabiliter esse compositum*), we properly call it sweet ... we must therefore acknowledge that, in the pleasure of those senses, what pertains to reason is that in which there is a certain rhythmic measure (*modulatio*).[28]

He proceeds to identify three sorts of sound, which include music as we would now recognize it and which the ear judges: 'sound in the utterance of an animate being, or sound in what breath produces in musical instruments, or sound in what is given forth by percussion', and comments:

> It [reason] saw the first class pertained to actors of tragedy and comedy or stage-players of this kind, and in fact all who give vocal renditions (*uoce propria canerent*); that the second class was restricted to flutes and similar instruments; and that to the third class were attributed the cithara, the lyre, cymbals, and

---

[25]*ord*. 2.12.35.
[26]Ibid.
[27]*ord*. 2.12.35.
[28]*ord*. 2.11.33.

everything that would be tonal on being struck (*omne quod percutiendo canorum esset*).[29]

But Augustine is insistent that these different types of sound are only useful – in other words, they only communicate something – when they are ordered according to the rules of number: 'Reason saw, however, that this material was of very little value, unless the sounds were arranged in a fixed measure of time (*certa dimensione temporum*) and in modulated variation of high and low pitch (*et acuminis grauitatisque moderata uarietate soni figurarentur*)'.[30] What Augustine is describing, of course, is what for him and all the ancients characterizes verse or poetry: metre, rhythm and pitch. 'In Latin', he observes 'this can be called nothing other than number (*numerus*). Thus, poets were begotten of reason'.[31] It is through number, then, that poets communicate not only sound to the hearing but also realities (*non solum sonorum, sed etiam uerborum rerumque magna momenta*), which are divine and eternal, for Augustine concludes:

> Reason understood, therefore, that in this fourth step of ascent – whether in particular rhythm or in modulation in general – numeric proportions held sway (*siue in rhythmis, siue in ipsa modulatione intelligebat regnare numeros*) and produced the finished product. With the utmost diligence it investigated as to what their nature might be, and, chiefly because by their aid it had elaborated all the aforesaid developments [its ascent through the liberal arts thus far], it concluded that they were divine and eternal.[32]

In *De ordine*, therefore, Augustine sets poetry apart as the particular form of measured, rhythmic sound which is superior to others because it is the one most clearly based on number, and

---

[29]*ord.* 2.14.39 We find the same three categories in *doc. Chr.* 6.17.27 as an explanation of the origin of the nine Muses (three statues were commissioned by three sculptors 'not.... because someone had seen three Muses in a dream, or because so many had appeared to anyone's eyes, but because it is easy to see that all sound which furnishes material for songs is of a three-fold nature'.

[30]*ord.* 2.14.40.

[31]Ibid.

[32]Ibid. 2.14. 41.

concludes that it is in and through the sound of verse (rhythm and/
or pitch) that meaning (divine and eternal number) is heard and
communicated.[33]

Augustine does not, therefore, dismiss sensuous, performed music,
whether vocal, instrumental or percussive, which, as he puts it, 'flows
into the past and is imprinted on the memory',[34] but he makes it
clear that what is important is the divine and eternal number which
structures it and which it signifies. In the *De ordine*, the liberal
art of music is therefore *both* a matter of theory and practice, of
number and of verse, of the mind and the body, reason and voice.
As Augustine concludes, music is a 'branch of learning [which]
partakes as well of sense as of intellect' (*Unde ista disciplina sensus
intellectusque particeps Musicae nomen inuenit*).[35] Towards the end
of this chapter we will need to discuss more fully just how sense
does relate to intellect; in other words, how it is that sensuous music
signifies, but we can only do that in the light of a careful reading of
Augustine's own attempt to address this question, in the work he
devoted specifically to the liberal art of music: his *De musica*.

Readers who have any familiarity with early Christianity will
be aware that, in outlining the two senses of music in the ancient
world – the rational discipline and sensuous performance – I have
also begun to touch on two poles of early Christian life and thought:
that of the educated and uneducated, the philosopher bishop and the
layperson, theory and practice, reason and faith, the soul and body.
These polarities run through the early Church like geographical
fissures, stratifying people and their social and ecclesial structures
and practices. They are the fault lines of asceticism; the tectonic
plates which slowly but inexorably shift to create whole new
continents of thinking and of practice. It is one such shift which I will
begin exploring here, by examining how classical ideas of music and
meaning, such as we saw Marrou rehearsing, were transformed into
a theology of music by someone like the fourth-/fifth-century bishop
of Hippo, Augustine. It is not for nothing that Augustine has been
called the architect of Western Christendom, and I would like to
suggest that this is at least in part due to his extraordinary rethinking
of the discipline and practice of music in a Christian context.

---

[33]*ord.* 2.14.41.
[34]2.14.41.
[35]2.14.41.

There actually isn't a great deal of scholarly work on the *De musica*,[36] despite the fact that it is the only early Christian treatise devoted to music before Boethius, Cassiodorus and Isidore of Seville, in the fifth-seventh centuries, made it something of a Christian genre. When scholars do turn to it they tend, for obvious reasons, to hastily pass over the abstract, technical stuff of books 1–5: these books have little immediate interest for the theologian, untrained in classical metre (to be honest, unless you know what a *trochaic tetrameter catalectic* is, a good deal of it does indeed go over your head!)[37] and seem to be wholly unexceptional for the classicist[38] – indeed scholarly judgements of Augustine's abilities in this area have been somewhat scathing.[39] But I am persuaded that Augustine doesn't do anything without reason: that he isn't writing primarily as an educator, musicologist or philosopher but as a newly converted Christian. The first five books of this work, along with other early works which smack too much of the schoolroom, should not just be written off as a preliminary *exercitatio animi* – an 'exercise of the mind', or flexing of the intellectual muscles, so to speak, to enable it to grasp the hard truths which will be presented later (it might well be this, but that is important in itself).[40] Rather, I think that if Augustine takes the classical understanding of poetry and the liberal art of music seriously then we should too.[41]

---

[36]Though there is recent work from a musicological angle (e.g. Wulf (2013)). For a survey of the history of scholarship, see Jeserich (2013) 53–57; for bibliography on *De musica* see Bettetini (1991) 430–469.

[37]Though Blackwood (2015) does an extraordinary job at introducing the uninitiated to the technicalities of poetic metre for theological purposes.

[38]Which is probably why it hasn't often been translated.

[39]Marrou (1958) 272–273, for example, comments, 'En realité plus on l'approfondit, plus on s'aperçoit que la théorie du rhythme selon s. Augustin est boiteuse et incomplète.... Augustin a voulu écrier un traité de rhythmique mais les forces lui ont manqué. Lu attentivement, son ouvrage ne suppose presque aucune érudition specifiquement musicale.'

[40]E.g. Marrou (1958) 299–327.

[41]Though see *ep.* 101 (408/9), where Augustine retrospectively judges books 1–5 far less important than book 6, commenting that they are 'very difficult to understand' and 'hardly worth knowing and reading by our son and fellow deacon, Julian, since he is now fighting with us in Christ's army'. He describes book 6, on the other hand (the only one he corrected and sent to Memorius, who had requested the work) as the 'fruit of the rest [of the work]', *ep.* 101.4.

'Birds do it'[42]

Augustine begins his *De Musica* in the most unpromising way
possible for anyone in search of something on actual music – by
which I mean music sounded and heard. The emphasis appears
to be firmly upon the rational quality of music. As we saw in the
introduction, he defines music as follows: *musica est scientia bene
modulandi*; music is a knowledge (*scientia*) of how to measure
(*modulandi*) well (*bene*) (1.2.2).[43] The element of 'fittingness',
however, which the word *bene* comprehends, gives the lie to
any thoroughgoing rationalism and draws our attention to the
important fact that the liberal art of music was never 'just' a matter
of knowledge or *scientia*. Like all the liberal arts, it was understood
as an articulation of the nature of reality. As such, music was studied
not just as a way of expressing quantitative judgements about the
nature of number/rhythm. As we have already seen in Augustine's
earlier *De ordine*, where music appears as the fourth stage in an
ascent through the liberal arts, at the point at which reason turns
from the arts in which reason is discovered through discourse to the
arts in which reason is discovered through pleasure, music was also
studied in order to make qualitative judgements about the truth
which number embodies and its ethical and aesthetic aspects.[44] It is
these we will be examining in this chapter.

In this first book, however, Augustine is quick to follow his
philosophical predecessors in making clear that performed music –
song and dance (since the latter is also based on rhythmic movement
and is, in Habinek's terms, a form of 'ritualised speech') – is no
more and no less than a matter of imitation, memory, practice and
acquired skill: it belongs to the realm of the senses; to unthinking

---

[42]Louis Armstrong 'Let's fall in love'.

[43]*mus.* 1.2.2.

[44]von Balthasar (1984) 116–117 '[number] cannot be regarded as mere quantification
of being or merely a translation into mathematics, because the unity which these
numbers and numerical relations reflect is, beyond all quantity, the qualitative as
such'; Pickstock (1998) 196, 'To say that the essence of beauty is in number.... sounds
to us like an attempt to reduce aesthetics to science and formal rules. However,
this would be to neglect the fact that for the tradition, number had a qualitative
dimension and a mysterious, inexhaustible depth. The break-up of this tradition in
fact generated the duality of science and art.'

and unconscious imitation. The fact that it is shared by birds, who do not possess reason, as well as singers or instrumental players, dancers and actors, who do, but evidently aren't using it, indicates that in their activity as performers, reason has no role to play: they perform primarily to gain money and renown.[45] That he cannot bring himself to call them 'musicians' – this term belongs to the one who has acquired an intellectual grasp of the discipline of music through rigorous study[46] – says it all. So performed music – song and dance – seems to be dismissed from the outset as unhelpful and unworthy of further consideration. As the Master confirms for the pupil in book 1, 'many things in singing and dancing are reprehensible, and ... if we take the word mensuration (*modulationis nomen*) from them, the almost divine art becomes degraded'.[47]

However – for there is, thankfully, an however – amidst the ensuing, arduous trawl through the liberal art of music and the technicalities of classical metre, in books 1–5 of *De musica*, the dialogue is punctuated by moments when Augustine and his interlocutor stop to reflect and to consider a number of matters which I think might usefully detain us, too, as they seem to give the lie to his peremptory dismissal of performed music. The first is what Augustine calls 'a natural sense of hearing'; the second is the related question of how the immutable truths of music are given sensuous form; and the third is the nature of authority.

A natural sense of hearing

Whatever it is, through which we approve or disapprove, not by reason but by nature (*non ratione sed natura*), when something sounds, I call the rhythm of the sense itself ... the natural, so to speak judicial power (*naturalis uero illa uis quasi iudiciaria*), which is present in the ears, does not cease to exist in silence, nor is it the sound that brings it to us; rather, it is the sound that is received by it to be either approved or disapproved of.[48]

---

[45]*mus.* 1.4.5–1.6.12 Or worse, in immoral contexts, with immoral ends. Augustine's criticism of pagan music is a commonplace among Christian writers: e.g. *ciu.* 2.4.
[46]*mus.* 1.6.12.
[47]*mus.* 1.2.3 Cf *ord.* 1.4.5; 2.18.48–19.50.
[48]*mus.* 6.2.3.

The natural sense of hearing is one that Augustine appeals to each time he and his pupil/interlocutor pause in their discussion, so that one of them can actually read out or give voice to the verses they are discussing. He describes it as a judgement of the senses (*iudicandum ... sensus*) or a judgement of the ear (*iudicium aurium*), a judgement of natural and common sense (*naturali et communi sensu iudicaret*) shared by all.[49]

Marrou takes a superior, cultured high ground and suggests that this natural sense of hearing is in fact one of the reasons for Augustine's rejection of performed music: it is precisely because it is a matter of sense rather than reason – something which is shared by everyone, educated and uneducated, that it is therefore inimical to a philosophical culture.[50] In fact, Augustine's *De musica* demonstrates that just the opposite is the case. By regularly reading the verse they are discussing aloud to each other, in books 1–5 of *De musica*, the Master and his pupil are both given a chance to hear and to listen to the verse's rhythms as they are performed in and across time, by the voice, so that they reverberate in their ears.[51]

Here is one example of many similar exchanges, taken from book two:

Magister (Master): ... listen to these verses:
Volo tandem tibi parcas, labor est in chartis,
et apertum ire per auras animum permittas.
placet hoc nam sapienter remittere interdum
aciem rebus agendis decenter intentam.

---

[49]*mus.* 2.12.23 *sensu.... iudices; iudicandum.... sensus;* 3.3.5 *iudicium aurium;* 3.7.16 *aurium iudicio;* 4.16.30 *naturali et communi sensu iudicaret;* 4.17.37 *audiendo natura communis* 6.4.5 *naturali iudicio sentiendi.... quasi quandam naturali iure ferre sententiam.* Clark (2017) e.g. 431–432; 438 does not mention this natural sense of hearing but suggests that Augustine chose not to use classical metre when he composed a song/poem himself (the *Psalm against the Donatists; Psalmus contra partem Donati*) because it was effectively elitist and only accessible to those educated in the liberal arts; that he preferred words to rhythmical sound/music. *De musica* is rather different.

[50]Marrou (1958) 202: 'Elle [la musique] est réservée à l'élite, refusée à la masse. Si la musique n'était que le jeu plaisant des son, le même instinct qui y conduit l'oiseau y conduirait aussi l'*imperita multitude*: Augustin le sait par expérience, rien n'est plus répandu qu'une oreille naturellement musicale. De là le souci de s'évader vers la science'.

[51]e.g. *mus.* 2.12.23; 2.13.25.

Discipulus (Pupil): That is enough.

M. Too true, for these verses I was forced to compose on the
spur of the moment are pretty rude. And yet I want to know
the judgement your sense (*iudicium sensus tui*) passes in the
case of these four, too.

D. And here again what else is there to say except that they
sounded correct and smooth?
[The Master then tries to make a point about the possibility
of mixing and combining six-time feet]

M. ... your own sense of hearing can judge (*ita sensu interrogato
iudices licet*) any six-time foot capable of substitution for
any other six-time foot ...[he gives an example]

D. I have them.

M. Then put them together and recite them, or better, listen
to me recite them so that your sense of hearing may be
freer of its time for judging (*quo ad iudicandum liberior
sensus uacet*). For to introduce the equality of a continued
number without offending your ears, I shall give the whole
combination three times ... [he does this] You don't find
anything in this flow of feet, do you, to rob your ears of
equality and smoothness?

D. Not at all.

M. Were you pleased, then? Although in this kind of thing it
logically follows what does not offend delights.

D. I can't say I have been affected otherwise than you expect.

M. Then your decision is, all these six-time feet can with
propriety be combined and mixed.

D. It is.[52]

When Augustine sent a copy of *De musica* to bishop Memorius in
408/9, it is precisely this process which he recommends to him as a
reader: he tells him that he should read the work aloud – especially
the first five books – in order to distinguish the speakers and to 'sound
the lengths of the syllables by pronouncing them aloud. For only in
that way can the different kinds of metre be expressed and impressed
upon the sense of hearing.'[53] Augustine therefore clearly anticipates

---

[52]*mus.* 2.12.22–23.
[53]*ep* 101.3.

that Memorius will imitate the master and pupil of the dialogue, for it is on the basis of actually perceiving number/rhythm with the senses – whether this be listening to a verse being read or a beat being clapped, watching a hand being raised and lowered to indicate an upbeat and downbeat (*arsis/thesis*),[54] seeing someone dancing (or, indeed a combination of these actions) that the natural sense of hearing is able to say whether a particular metre works, whether it sounds right or wrong. What Augustine describes makes one think of Lully or Rameau, with a baroque orchestra and troupe of dancers, conducting by beating time with a stick: 'Now, fix your ears on the sound and your eyes on the beats. For the hand beating time is not to be heard but seen, and note must be taken of the amount of time given to the arsis [the upbeat] and thesis [the downbeat].'[55]

The natural sense judges, then, not in reference to the laws or rules the master and his pupil discuss with such technical precision but on the simple basis of whether what is heard or seen occasions delight and pleasure, or offence and dismay, for the perceiver:

M: And suppose an instrument struck in rhythm, with one
       sound a time's length and the next double repeatedly and
       connectedly, to make what are called iambic feet, and
       suppose someone dancing (*saltet*) to it moving his limbs in
       time. Then could you not give the time's measure (*modulum
       temporum*), explain the movement's intervals alternating as
       one to two, either in the beats (*plausu*) heard or the dancing
       seen? Or if you could not tell the numbers in its measure,
       wouldn't you at least delight in the rhythm you sense?
D: It is as you say. For those who know these numbers and
       discern them in the beats and dancing easily identify them.
       And those who don't know them and can't identify them
       admit, nevertheless, they get a certain pleasure from them.[56]

---

[54]*mus.* 2.10.18 'In making a beat, since the hand is raised or lowered, the arsis claims one part of the foot, the thesis the other.'

[55]2.13.24; 4.11.12 'and they will judge this easily by your repeating them and beating them with the necessary rests'.

[56]*mus.* 1.13.27. Cf. *mus.* 2.2.2; 2.12.23; 2.13.25. *mus.* 3.7.16 'For we have seen whatever is expressed in the ratio of numbers (*numerorum ratione*), which are in no way deceptive, is capable of delighting the ear.... listen as I keep repeating *Quae canitis sub antris*, and charm your senses with its numerical quality.'

Delight in number is therefore a judgement of sense, not reason. As we have already noted, Augustine made this point clearly in his earlier *De ordine*,[57] in relation to hearing and seeing, when he observed:

> Insofar as we have been able to investigate, we now detect certain traces of reason in the senses, and, with regard to sight and hearing, we find it in pleasure itself .... With regard to the eyes, that is usually called beautiful in which the harmony of parts is wont to be called reasonable ... in the pleasure of the senses, what pertains to reason is that in which there is a certain rhythmic measure.[58]

He makes it clear that this is a judgement which anyone can make: the pupil as well as the master, the unlearned and the learned, the one who knows the rules and the one who is ignorant of them, the performer and the audience, simply on the basis of hearing or seeing. Of the performer, he comments: 'What good singer, even though he be unskilled in the art of music, would not, by the same natural sense, keep in his singing both the rhythm and melody known to memory? And what can be more subject to measure than this? The uninstructed man has no knowledge of it. Nevertheless, he does it by nature's doing.'[59] Likewise, of the hearer, he observes: 'And so when something is sung or recited having a determinate ending, more than one foot, and a natural motion pleasing the senses by a certain equableness even before consideration of the numbers involved, then it is already metre.'[60]

The idea of a natural sense is one that does not disappear from Augustine's thinking: in *De trinitate* he uses it again to discuss the concord of Christ's single death and resurrection with our own double death and resurrection, in body and soul. His comments give us an exciting glimpse of what his projected treatise on melody or harmony, which would have been a companion volume to *De musica*'s treatment of rhythm, might have contained:

---

[57]*ord.* 2.11.33.
[58]*ord.* 2.11.33.
[59]*ord.* 2.19.49. Cf. *en.Ps.* 128.1 – as a dancer moves their arms and legs to music, so those who follow God's law dance to its rhythm.
[60]*mus.* 3.8.19.

This match – or agreement or concord or consonance or whatever the right word is for the proportion of one to two (*haec enim congruentia, siue conuenientia, vel concinentia, uel consonantia*) – is of enormous importance in every construction (*compaginatione*) or interlock (*coaptatione*) – that is the word I want – of creation. What I mean by this interlock (*coaptationem*), it has just occurred to me, is what the Greeks call *harmonia* (ἁρμονίαν).[61]

Evidently, what he has in mind is not just poetic rhythm but the harmony of singing voices, which everyone who performs and hears can instinctively judge. Thus, he observes, that this consonance is

found extensively in us, and is so naturally ingrained in us (and who by, if not by him who created us?), that even the unskilled feel it whether singing themselves or listening to others. It is what makes concord between high pitched and deep voices (*uoces acutiores grauioresque concordant*), and if anyone strays discordantly away from it, it is not our knowledge (*scientiam*), which many lack, but our very sense of hearing (*ipsum sensum auditus nostri*) that is painfully offended.[62]

Augustine's natural sense of hearing is thus what we might describe as an intuitive judgement: we intuitively respond with pleasure to something that sounds harmonious and rhythmical and are offended when we hear a discordant, dissonant noise.[63] He describes the former when he observes that, even when we cannot accurately judge whether a time is 'single' or 'double', we can be 'delighted by the harmony (*congruentia delectari*) and pleasurably affected (*voluptate affici*)'[64] and alludes to the latter when he refers to 'the shock the ear feels' when the metre which it has delighted in are placed in a different order. [65]

---

[61]*trin.* 4.2.4 *coaptatio* appears to be a word invented by Augustine in this context to express the sense of accurate joining together suggested by the Greek ἁρμονία.
[62]*trin.* 4.2.4.
[63]*mus.* 4.16.34 'Now, insofar as the senses are concerned, they have done their duty in this question, and have indicated what they would approve and what they would not.'
[64]*mus.* 1.13.27.
[65]*mus.* 4.11.12–13.

If this is the case, a number of questions follow: where does this instinct come from?; how do we acquire it?; how does it relate to the judgement of reason? and how does it square with Augustine's criticism of performed music as merely a matter of imitation and practice? He doesn't ask these questions in books 1–5 but rather takes the ability to instinctively judge what is heard very much as a 'given', which does not need or merit further reflection. The fact that he can do so is a measure of how far this idea of a natural sense of hearing was an intrinsic and accepted part of the philosophical and rhetorical tradition in which he stands: it is used by his long-time mentor, Cicero; by the master of rhetorical teaching, Quintilian, and both, David van Dusen suggests, probably ultimately owe this idea to Aristotle and Aristoxenus.[66] We will have to wait until book 6 before Augustine begins to address the sort of questions it provokes for us, and when he does, the results are quite extraordinary.

There are, however, a few notable exceptions to an unquestioning acceptance of the natural sense of hearing as a 'given', in the first part of *On Music*, and it is striking that the passages in which they occur make the same point: that it is through the senses that immutable truth is apprehended by human beings.

The secret sanctuaries of music

Towards the end of book 1 of *De musica* Augustine turns to consider the origin of music and how we perceive it through the senses: he describes music as 'issuing forth from the most secret sanctuaries' (*procedens quodammodo de secretissimis penetrabilibus musica*) and then leaving 'traces (*uestigia*) in our very senses or in things sensed by us'.[67] The question is how we follow the traces to arrive at their source. When Augustine suggests that we do so by discussing

---

[66]Van Dusen (2014) refers to what he calls a '"sensualist" commonplace in Cicero's rhetorical treatises' (205), whereby versification originates in *sensus* not in *ratio* (213) and to an 'Aristoxenian-Ciceronian *iudicium sensus* – possibly traceable to Augustine's exposure, in Carthage, to Aristotle's Latin Categories' (211–212). Cicero uses the term *aurium mensura* (*orat.* III.47.183); Quintilian, *aurium iudicium* (*Inst. orat.* 9.4.118). Cf BA 7 note complémentaire 33.

[67]*mus.* 1.13.28 Cf *ord.* 2.15.43 where Augustine observes that reason tends to look to the 'shadows and vestiges' (*umbras.... atque uestigia*) of number in things perceived by the senses, rather than the liberal art of music or the numbers themselves.

'the short interval lengths which delight us in singing and dancing' (*his brevibus intervallorum spatiis quae in cantando saltandoque nos mulcent*)[68] he is making explicit two interesting features of the 'natural sense of hearing': first, that immutable truths (music in the secret sanctuary) need sensual expression (in the vestiges apprehended by the senses); second, that this sensual expression, as it were, makes the infinite and eternal nature of music accessible to us by confining it, or capturing it, so to speak, in short, measured, rhythmic intervals which the senses can easily apprehend and which instinctively occasion its delight.[69] We might well conclude, then, that for Augustine performed music is no more and no less than a necessary constraint: it needs to be sounded if the truths of number are to be apprehended by human ears.[70]

The authority of the ancients

The other exception to the tendency to take the natural sense of hearing simply as a given, which also reveals the necessity of sense perception and sensuous music, relates to the fact that each time the natural sense of hearing is invoked in *De musica*, questions relating to what Augustine calls 'the authority of the ancients' tend to follow. This is partly because he is aware that the judgement of the ears is very much shaped by this authority, in other words, by the traditions and customs which the ancient poets and grammarians established and which have subsequently had a determining influence on the way in which human beings not only practise the rhythmic arts but also how they hear and judge them. However, while acknowledging its force, and while

---

[68]Ibid.

[69]Augustine makes a similar contrast between 'sensible traces' and the 'real places where it [music] is free of all body' at the end of book 5 when he comments: 'Let this be the end of the discussion, so we may next come with as much wisdom as we can from these sensible traces of music (*ab his uestigiis ejus sensibilibus*), all dealing with that part of it in the numbers of the times, to the real places (*ipsa cubilia*) where it is free of all body' (5.13.28).

[70]Cf *ord.* 2.5.14 'Now in music, in geometry, in the movements of the stars, in the fixed ratios of numbers (*in numerorum necessitatibus*), order reigns in such manner that if one desires to see its source and its very shrine, so to speak, he either finds it in these, or he is unerringly led to it through them.'

generally conceding that it should be observed and accepted, Augustine is ambivalent about the 'authority of the ancients', not least because it can sometimes appear to be at odds with reason: it rests on what he describes as 'inveterate habit' (2.1.1 – *inueterata consuetudo*); 'the inveterate will of men' (5.5.10 – *inveterata voluntas hominum*), on 'custom' (3.2.3; 5.10.20 – *consuetudine*), arbitrary 'names' (3.2.3 – *nominibus*) and sometimes on 'false' and 'irrational opinion' (5.5.9 – *irrationabili opinione*) rather than reason (3.2.4; 5.10.20 – *ratio*) or immutable truths (3.2.3 – *rebus*).[71] The question he and his interlocutor therefore face is: what should they do when the conventions and authorities which now inevitably inform their natural judgement – those conventions which have been agreed, taught, handed down and practised from one generation of poets or grammarians, and their hearers, to the next, so that they have become a matter of history and belief (4.16.30–31) – differ from a purely rational apprehension of the rules of number? Augustine's response is, I think, fascinating: he argues that the authority of the ancients should be upheld and observed precisely *because* it has become a matter of commonly accepted practice and custom. As he comments repeatedly in these first five books:

> It is not proper when they [the poets] have fixed them [the laws of metre] by reasoning (*ratione fixerint*), to make any change in them, even if we could make the change according to reasoning (*secundum rationem*) and without any offence to the ear. And the knowledge of this sort of thing is handed on, not by art but by history (*non arte, sed historia traditur*). And therefore, it is believed rather than known. For if some Falerian or other has composed metres to sound like these ... we can't know it, but only believe it by hearing and reading (*sed tantummodo credere audiendo et legendo*)[72]
> ... the poet's wishing these numbers to be unchangeable when we use this metre has to be respected. For it satisfies the ear ... in this metre then, nothing will be changed, not for the reason

[71]Augustine is presenting the contrast in classical terms as one between *res* and *signa* and no doubt anticipating his distinction between *enjoyment* and *use* in book 6, in a matter which foreshadows his extended development of these ideas in *doc. Chr.* Book 1.
[72]Ibid. 4.16.30.

by which we avoid inequality, but for that by which we observe authority.[73]

There therefore appears to be a contrast between judgement based on authority and judgement based on reason. The former is apparent in both the poet and the grammarian, in their different ways: for example, in *mus*. 3.3.5, the pupil comments:

> You don't seem to remember you have already sufficiently distinguished the difference between the grammarian and the musician when I told you I didn't possess the knowledge of long and short syllables, a knowledge passed down by grammarians. Unless, perhaps you let me show the rhythm in beats and not in words. For I don't deny I am capable of ear-judgments for regulating the values of times. But as to what syllables are to be pronounced long or short, since it's a matter of authority, I am altogether ignorant.

What he readily acknowledges as the ancients' authority – both the ear-judgements of the poet and musician, as well as the teaching of the grammarians – cannot, then, be overturned or shrugged off. The weight of conventional practice and learning has an authority not just because it is taught as a matter of rules but precisely because it has become tradition: the expected and anticipated way to do things and one which has undeniably shaped the natural sense of hearing and the way in which it hears and judges. As he observes of the names we use to refer to different types of verse: 'because the old names (*uetusta uocabula*) are not to be despised and custom (*consuetudine*) should not be lightly violated unless it is opposed to reason, we should use the names of feet the Greeks instituted, now in use among the Latins',[74] and similarly in relation to the natural sense itself: 'in the measuring of verse the inveterate will of man (*inueterata uoluntas hominum*) and not the eternal ratio of things is to be considered, since we first perceive its measured length

---

[73]Ibid. 4.16.31; Cf 5.1.1. These comments echo what Augustine observes in the *Confessions* about the way in which children learn a language: it is primarily a matter of imitation, based on tradition, custom and authority, not a matter of reason or rules.

[74]Ibid. 2.8.15.

naturally by the ear (*prius naturaliter aure sentiamus*), and then establish it by the rational consideration of numbers'.[75]

There is an interesting parallel to the arguments we have just discovered in *De musica* for taking the instinctive judgement of the natural sense and the authority of ancients seriously, in book 3 of the *Confessions* (3.7.12–14). Considering the rather disconcerting behaviour of the Old Testament patriarchs, Augustine is forced to admit that there is a striking gap between the customs of their time and the unchanging, eternal law of God – or what he calls, the 'norm of righteousness'. Interestingly, for our purposes, he uses the analogy of his own composition of songs according to the self-consistent, unvarying art of poetry, while observing the rules for the placing of metrical feet agreed by custom and convention, and concludes, in relation to the patriarchs, that 'justice ....unvaryingly self-consistent, does not impose its demands at once but adjusts and allots to different periods the provisions most apt for them'.[76] So temporal customs might differ from the immutable rules and indeed fall short of them, but they are nonetheless acceptable and understandable in terms of their own age. We find a similar contrast in Augustine's later, systematic, consideration of the role of human culture in the second book of his *De doctrina Christiana* (*On Christian Doctrine*). Here, considering what he calls the 'things instituted by men (*rerum quas instituerunt homines*)',[77] (in contrast to those which are of divine institution), he identifies those human institutions which are not superstitious, superfluous or self-indulgent but which are necessary and useful – which depend not on a 'natural meaning' (*natura*) but on human 'institution and consent' (*instituto et consensione hominum*)[78]. These include such necessary and useful human institutions as 'the forms of letters without which we cannot read, and a sufficient variety of languages', [79] as well as the not so necessary, but unharmful, signs made by the public crier, in order to explain the movements of actors when dancing or miming. All of these signs only signify because of human consent –

---

[75]Ibid. 5.5.10.
[76]*conf.* 3.7.14.
[77]*doc. Chr.* 2.19.29 He offers the definition: 'all practices which have value among men because men agree among themselves that they are valuable are human institutions' (2.25.38).
[78]Ibid. 2.25.38; 2.25.38 'signs are not valid among men except by common consent'.
[79]Ibid. 2.26.40.

'signs are not valid among men except by common consent'[80] – and like superstitious practices, they can therefore vary according to human agreement, according to custom and practice: 'Therefore, just as all of these significations move men's minds in accordance with the consent of their societies, and because this consent varies, they move men differently, nor do men agree upon them because of an innate value, but they have a value because they are agreed upon.'[81]

What Augustine is identifying here is the importance of the ties that bind us: the tacit, customary and relative agreements of human individuals and social groupings, in particular times and places, as well as eternal laws. It will become clear as *De musica* progresses (and especially in book 6) that what characterizes human agreement and custom is largely due to the Fall, and yet even this, he will argue, is comprehended by God's ordered providence. In the *De ordine* Augustine observes that fallen human beings cannot see the beautiful work of divine providence. From their limited, temporal perspective, they can only glimpse a part, rather than the whole. Nevertheless, he argues, it is providence that orders our sinfulness and makes it part of the divine order. In other words, God can use our customs and traditions, whether fallen or simply temporal: the behaviour of the patriarchs, the conventions of the poets, the rules of the grammarians, the sound of verse or music, the judgement of the ear, by ordering them according to his providence. They become, as it were, a necessary (providential) constraint.[82]

To return to *De musica*: it is clear that in these early books Augustine is persuaded that to ignore authority and tradition would be to introduce a disorientating confusion into human affairs, which clearly requires the 'authority of the ancients' in order to function – even if, being a matter of human invention,

---

[80]Ibid. 2.25.38.

[81]Ibid. 2.24.37.

[82]Cf Isidore of Pelusium in McKinnon (1987) 123 'If the Holy One tolerated blood and sacrifice because of the childishness of men at that time, why do you wonder that the music of cithara and psaltery was used, which, as some say, heals the passions of the soul and alleviates pain, soothes anger and assuages grief through tears.' Here, then, music joins the customs and conventions of human practices as a necessary, providential concession to human weakness.

habit and custom, it proves to be fallible.[83] Again, then, it is in time and through the senses – through authority, tradition, history, faith, habit and custom – that the immutable ratios of music are made known to human beings. We will have to wait until book 6 for the theological implications of these insights to be drawn out.

Having read books 1–5 of *De Musica*, the reader emerges with two rather conflicting understandings of music: it consists of the laws and rules of rhythm/number but it is to be appreciated and judged 'in performance', as it were: by being sounded and heard. As Augustine puts it succinctly in book 5: the senses announce and reason judges; *sensu nuntio, indice ratione*.[84] Even the erudite and learned (such as the Master in the dialogue) need music to be performed before they can judge according to the eternal, immutable rules which they have acquired through study. The unlearned, by contrast, need the erudite to compose verses and to perform them in order that they, too, might hear and apprehend the rhythms with their ears and eyes, if not with their intellects, and appreciate them through the delight and pleasure they occasion. As Augustine observes in relation to the examples he has given of the 568 different poetic metres:

> Although these examples we have given and those we can give, poets judged proper in making them, and common nature in hearing them (*in audiendo natura communis*), yet unless a learned and practiced man's recitation should commend them to our ears, and the sense of hearing (*sensusque audientium*) should not be slower than humanity requires, the ones we have treated cannot be judged true.[85]

---

[83]Cf *doc. Chr.* 4 (e.g. 4.20.41) where Augustine demonstrates his acute sensitivity to the rhetorical conventions of his time, to the extent that Scripture, or his own work and preaching, does not seem 'right' unless it has, for example, the correct rhythmic closings (*clausulae*) for a phrase. It is partly a matter of rules, but much more, of convention and custom, expected and anticipated by both speaker and hearer. The force of such conventions is seen in his inability to ignore them, even though they rather undermine what he has to say about the role of rhetoric in a Christian context.
[84]*mus.* 5.1.1.
[85]*mus.* 4.17.37 Cf *mus.* 4.16.30 'half taught men could see this, if it were recited and beaten out by a learned man according to both laws. For they would judge from natural and common sense (*naturali et communi sensu iudicarent*) what the discipline's norm would prescribe.'

We should also note that the learned and the unlearned alike must also observe authority and tradition, for they provide the only context in which their respective 'judgements' can make any sense.

Already, then, the rather stark separation between music as a rational discipline and music in practice is beginning to be broken down and it has happened for a number of salient reasons: it has become clear that poetry or music is not just a matter for the intellect but is best apprehended and judged – by both the erudite and the unlearned – by being sounded and heard. The learned can then judge rationally, but they are aided by the instinctive judgement of sense; the unlearned can then judge instinctively on the basis of delight and pleasure. Both depend on a natural sense of hearing, and on authority and tradition, which have taught and handed down the rules to the one and (presumably) attuned the ears of both to be able to hear and appreciate them. There are therefore at least three things at play in the apprehension of music in Augustine's – so far – very classical presentation of it: an intellectual grasp of its laws, a natural sense of hearing, authority and tradition.

Book 6: A theology of music

Turning to book 6 the change of key is so marked that some scholars have felt it necessary to suggest that Augustine either revised it or at least added bits (such as the preface and conclusion) later. There is no evidence for this, apart from the need that such scholars evidently feel to explain what they are reluctant to acknowledge could be part of the early Augustine's mindset.[86]

The first thing to change is the poetry/music itself. All of the verses which Augustine selected to read, beat out and discuss with his pupil, in books 1–5, are taken either from classical authors or composed by Augustine himself. None of them are remotely Christian or scriptural. Hearing Augustine take and read out, for the first time, the opening

---

[86]Marrou (1958) 580–583 and O'Connell (1978) 66–67, for example, suggest that the introduction and conclusion to book 6 were emendations inserted by Augustine in 408/9, twenty years after the original composition. See Jacobsson (2017= CSEL 102) 1–10 for a discussion of the various theories and Jacobsson (2002) xxvii–xxviii for a counter-argument based on extant versions.

line of Ambrose of Milan's hymn, *Deus Creator Omnium*,[87] is rather like listening to the opening theme of Bach's *Musical Offering* – spare, simple but heavy with the weight of what is to come. *Deus Creator Omnium.* Why does Augustine suddenly cite a Christian poem – not just that, a Christian hymn? We should perhaps remember his comments in *ep.* 101, when he sent a copy of book 6 to Bishop Memorius, that he did not use the psalms in *De musica* because he does not know Hebrew, and furthermore, that he is aware that, although the psalms are written in metrical verse, 'the translator from the Hebrew language ... was not able to indicate the metre for fear that the demands of the metre would force him to depart from the truth in his translation more than the sense of the verses permitted'.[88] So, the most obvious religious poetry was not available to Augustine as verse.

We could also suggest, rather prosaically, that he uses a Christian hymn at this point in the work because he had just recently discovered it and perhaps even sung it: Ambrose had been a key figure in his conversion; he had catechized and baptized him in Milan in 387; he represented the intellectual Christian Augustine aspired to be able to reconcile classical learning and culture with Christian preaching and exegesis. Moreover, he was a musical innovator; it is to Ambrose that we owe what, in retrospect, we can appreciate is an entirely new form of Christian hymn.[89] As Gillian

---

[87]On Ambrose's hymns, Fontaine (ed.) (1992); Dunkle (2016). For the text of *Deus Creator Omnium*, with English translation, see Ramsay (1997) 170–171.

[88]*ep.* 101.4. Cf *doc.Chr.* 4.20.41 'the musical discipline where rhythm [i.e. number] is fully learned, is not lacking in our Prophets, for the most learned Jerome observes metre in some of them as they exist in the Hebrew tongue, although he has not translated them metrically because he wished to keep the verbal accuracy of his translation'.

[89]The evidence for early Christian hymnody before Ambrose is rather scattered and certainly not a substantial collection of texts. We can assume that from an early stage early Christians sang the Old Testament psalms, biblical canticles (listed in Stapert (2007) 164 n. 27–28) and hymns (the earliest of which may be embedded in a number of NT and apostolic texts (Lattke 1991); listed in Stapert (2007) 165 and Page (2010) chapter 3 and appendix). A very early Christian hymn is appended to the end of Clement of Alexandria's *The Teacher* (*Paidagogus, Sources Chrétiennes* 158.192–203). In addition, we possess a fragment of a hymn with rudimentary notation from Oxyrhynchus (P. Oxy. XV 1786 – three lines, with indications of pitch but not of rhythm); an evening hymn, the *Phos Hilaron*, to be sung at the lighting of the candles, which is referred to by Basil of Caesarea in the fourth

Clark observes, 'Instead of classical hexameters, which often require unusual vocabulary and word-order and syntax, he used a simple iambic dimeter (acatelectic) with stress accents. Most of these eight-syllable lines are self-contained statements; they are grouped in four line-stanzas, and in the hymns securely attributed to Ambrose there are no more than eight such stanzas.'[90] Ambrose's innovation was to maintain this same, fixed pattern for all of his hymns (Augustine tells us about four of them and it is thought that we can attribute at least ten others to him).[91] It is a pattern which is strikingly simple, readily memorized and easily adapted to chanting and antiphonal singing. It became the pattern for hymnody throughout the Middle Ages[92] and was, if we are to believe Augustine, an immediate success and very soon was enthusiastically accepted throughout the Church worldwide[93] (we will discuss this further in the next chapter). What was happening here?

---

century as having been in traditional use (*On the Holy Spirit* – 29.73 Anderson (1980) *Sources Chrétiennes* 17). There is also evidence of hymnody in the *Odes of Solomon* (Lattke (1979–86); heretical texts – Gnostics, Arius (Dunkle (2016) 24–26 for bibliography); Ephrem the Syrian (Dunkle (2016) 28–32 for bibliography); a few remaining fragments of Hilary of Poitier's *Liber Hymnorum* (Dunkle (2016) 32–36) – though Jerome judged them un-sing-able (*Commentary on Galatians – in Gal 2 pref* (*St. Jerome's Commentaries on Galatians, Titus, and Philemon*, trans. Thomas P. Scheck (Notre Dame, IN: University of Notre Dame Press, 2010) PL 26:380); the hymns of Prudentius, Sedulius, Ennodius and Venantius Fortunatus (White (2000) for translations and commentary). Unfortunately, we have no idea of the music which Ambrose's hymns were sung to, though as we noted above, there have been attempts to reconstruct it (Pérès, *Chants de l'Église Milanaise* Harmonia Mundi). Indeed, we have no Roman music from this period at all (Mountford (1964) 210). On theories of music in ancient Rome, see Wille (1967); Dunkle (2016) 14–18 for a brief but very informative survey of the origins of Christian hymnody and extensive bibliography. Cf also Gordley (2011); Lattke (1991); Page (2010); Quasten (1988); Stapert (2007); Simonetti (1952); Smith (2011); Westermeyer (1998).
[90]Clark (2017) 427.
[91]The four Augustine tells us about are: *Aeterna rerum Conditor; Deus Creator Omnium; Iam surgit hora tertia; Intende qui Regis Israel*. Fontaine (ed.) (1992). On Ambrose's hymns in Augustine, see Beyenka (1957). On Ambrose's originality, see Cunningham (1955) 509–514; Charlet (1985) 627 interestingly comments that 'Le Vulgate des Psaumes contient d'ailleurs certain versets décomposables en quatre membres octosyllabiques'.
[92]White (2000) 22.
[93]*conf*. 9.7.15 'in other parts of the world also many of your churches imitate the practice: indeed, nearly all of them'.

As I indicated at the beginning of this chapter, I would like
to argue that what is happening is not just a new and successful
innovation in Christian hymnody, which transposes and transforms
classical verse into a Christian hymn with theological themes,
readily accessible to the unlearned majority,[94] but that Augustine's
adoption of Ambrose's hymn in this particular context – and his
continued use of it at significant moments in his career – marks
the beginnings of a new theology of music, which was to give what
we have referred to as 'sensuous music' – music performed and
heard – a central role.

When Augustine sounds the first line of this hymn for his
interlocutor we can almost hear him saying it (perhaps, excitingly,
singing it) and beating out the metre: *Dĕūs crĕātŏr ōmnĭūm.*[95] We might
now reasonably expect him to proceed according to what has become
their established method – one they shared with generations of pupils
in the liberal arts – and to investigate whether the verse is correct or
incorrect, rhythmic or dissonant, pleasing or offensive. They might
well conclude, in this instance, that *Dĕūs crĕātŏr ōmnĭūm* is indeed
correct, rhythmic, pleasing verse – rather simple and unadventurous,
not a very interesting or informative example but perfectly acceptable.
But this isn't why he has cited it and the discussion doesn't progress
along these lines. Instead, there is something about this verse that

---

[94]Though as White (2000) 10 comments, in contrast to the more conventionally
classical verse of their Christian contemporaries, the simple metre of Ambrose's
Hymns and non-classical metre of Augustine's *Psalm against the Donatists* (*Psalmus
contra partem Donati* (see Chapter 2 below, for further discussion) are 'notable
exceptions'. Augustine tells us (*retr.* 1.20) that he avoided classical metre in his song
'lest the requirement of metre should force some words on me that were less well-
known to the general public'. Clark (2017) 435 observes: 'A classical *carmen* would
have presented Augustine's target audience with problems of vocabulary, grammar
and syntax, and metre.' We should not forget, however, as we have seen in examining
Augustine's understanding of a natural sense of hearing and the role of authority
and tradition, how much even the ears of the uneducated had become attuned to
the formalities of classical Latin and the rhythms of poetic metre, even if they could
not compose or analyse them themselves. We hear a Shakespeare play or a work by
Bach in the same way: we could not compose it but we can listen to and appreciate it.
For a rather unsparing judgement of Augustine's *Psalmus contra partem Donati*, see
Van der Meer (1961) 332. On the work, Vroom (1933). It was certainly an exercise
which he did not repeat.
[95]Hermanowicz (2004) 197 on the way in which the *Deus Creator Omnium*
demarcates the book's beginning, middle and end.

makes Augustine pause rather longer than just to voice, listen and judge. There is something about the hymn that prompts him to go further and to raise the sort of questions which the idea of a natural sense of hearing provoked for us. It appears that, for him, too, the natural sense of hearing, which he has so far happily deployed, can no longer be taken as a 'given'. Instead, he is returned to first principles. The reason, I think, is that a line of Christian poetry, a Christian hymn, heavy with theological content, which sounds the most fundamental of Christian beliefs – God, the Creator of All – is one that demands a different approach.[96] This approach is one that will become familiar in Augustine's work and it is one that most early Christian thinkers found themselves engaged in for at least two main reasons: first, to think through the ambivalent relation between Christianity and classical culture and secondly, to take seriously what it means to believe in a God who creates everything from nothing and who is therefore the source of all created, mutable, temporal reality, including, in this case, poetry or music.

As so often, Augustine begins from his own experience as a human being. As we shall see, it is in the light of his experience of the soul's perception of sound that he will be able to progress towards the source of this perception in God, the Creator of All: from microcosmic rhythm and harmony to macrocosmic rhythm and harmony, as it were.[97]

The psychology of musical perception

Thus, in book 6 of *De musica*, Augustine has the Master set out with his patient interlocutor (and one senses, by this stage, that it

---

[96]Its identification of the Christian God with the creator God was no doubt particularly resonant for the early Augustine in contrast to the Manichees' (and his own former) dualist rejection of this catholic Christian doctrine. The doctrine of God's creation from nothing is, arguably, the key Christian doctrine for the early Augustine and one that therefore lays the foundations for the rest of his theological reflections (Harrison (2006) 74–114). There is a long tradition of Christian verse and song against heretical doctrine and especially in response to the heretics' own use of these media (see White (2000) 13–18; Dunkle (2016) 24–26).

[97]Pickstock (1998) 15 and Walhout (1979) note that Augustine begins with psychology and experience, in other words with phenomenology, rather than ontology.

is just as well he or she is fictional) to systematically examine what is involved when human beings hear something: in this instance, what happens when we hear *Deus Creator Omnium* being sung or said. They proceed to analyse the stages of perception; to assign to each stage a name; to categorize, hierarchize and generally feel that they are getting somewhere in investigating what are, in reality, difficult and elusive questions: what do we hear?, how do we hear?, how do we become aware of what we hear?, how do we record and remember it?, how do we recollect it?, how, finally (the question he had asked first, in books 1–5, becomes the final and decisive question) do we judge it? I'm not sure how helpful the terms they arrive at actually are, except for the purposes of the argument here (Augustine doesn't, as far as I am aware, use them again in this form, though the process they describe is one that remains fixed in his thought). The stages by which the soul perceives sound, and moves from the corporeal to the incorporeal, are described as different types of rhythm or number:

> Therefore answer me, if you please, my friend, with whom I am now discussing, so that we may move on from the corporeal to the incorporeal: when we pronounce the verse *Deus Creator Omnium*, where do you think that these four iambs, of which it consists, and the twelve time-units are, that is to say, should we say that these rhythms are merely in the sound which is heard (*in sono*) or also in the hearer's sense (*in sensu audientis*), which belongs to the ears, or also in the activity of the pronouncing person (*in actu ... pronuntiantis*), or since the verse is known, also in our memory (*in memoria*)? (6.2.2)

or 'in the natural judgement of perception (*naturali iudicio sentiendi*), when we are delighted by the equality of rhythms or offended when a mistake is made in them' (6.4.5).

Augustine begins book 6, then, with a careful analysis of the five different categories, or levels, of number by which the soul perceives sound and ascends from what is heard to what is known or apprehended.[98] They are:

---

[98]The name of each level varies according the stage of the argument in book 6; the names Augustine finally arrives at in 6.8.20–22 are the ones given here.

Sonantes/sounding numbers (*in sono*) = sound which reverberates in the ears (6.8.22)

Occursores/occurring numbers (*in sensu audientis*) = the activity of the soul in the one who hears, towards the actions of the body. (Augustine cannot allow the body, which is lower, to have any action upon the soul, which is higher; thus it must always be the soul that is active in sense perception.[99] In this activity the soul either agrees or disagrees with the actions of the body; they are experienced by the soul as pleasure or pain, as a result of which it acts either with ease or with difficulty respectively.) (6.5.9–10)

Progressores/progressing numbers (*in actu pronuntiantis*) = the activity of the soul in the one who speaks (6.8.20)

Recordabiles/recordable numbers (*in memoria*) 6.8.22 = the activity of the soul in recording sound through mental images created in the memory. There are two levels: occurring rhythms in the memory, which are recent (6.8.21); memorized rhythms, which are older and can be retrieved by being recollected (6.8.22).

Sensuales/sensuous numbers (*naturali iudicio sentiendi*) (6.4.5; 6.8.23) = the natural sense of hearing, whereby sound is perceived as either pleasing or offensive (in 6.8.23 they are temporarily labelled *iudiciales*, but when the judicial numbers of rational judgement are placed above them (see below), they become *sensuales*.)

Later, as I have indicated, Augustine reconsiders these levels and adds a sixth type of number:

Iudiciales/judicial numbers (6.9.24) = the rational judgement of sound by reason, so that its eternal, immutable rules or laws are known and we are able to explain *why* something delights or offends and whether it is right or wrong to enjoy them.[100]

The ascent is conveniently summarized, once again in relation to Ambrose's *Deus Creator Omnium*, towards the middle of book 6: 'When this verse, which we put forth, is sung .... We both hear it with occurring rhythms, and recognize it with the memorized rhythms, and pronounce it with the progressing rhythms, and enjoy it with these judicial [sensuous] rhythms, and evaluate it with some others [judicial rhythms].'[101] In so doing, 'we are examining' as Augustine puts it:

---

[99]*mus.* 6.5.9–11.
[100]For an account of similar ascents in the early works see Harrison (2006) 35–73.
[101]*mus.* 6.8.23.

The motions and states of one and the same nature, that is to say, the soul ... as it is one thing to be moved towards the reactions of the body, which occurs in perceiving, another to move oneself towards the body, which occurs in an activity, yet another thing to retain what has been produced in the soul as a result of these motions, which is to remember, so it is one thing to approve or disapprove of these motions, when they are first set in motion or when they are revived by remembrance, which occurs in the pleasure of that which is convenient and in the dismay of that which is inappropriate in such motions or reactions, and another thing to evaluate whether it is right or not to enjoy these things, which is done by reasoning.[102]

It takes the interlocutors quite a while to arrive at this point and a certain amount of chopping and changing (especially, and predictably, in relation to the most difficult levels: at the beginning (in sound) and at the end (in judgement)). The names might seem a bit off-putting, but they are doing something that allows us to get an overall view of ancient ideas of sense perception; to actually address some of the questions which arose when we encountered the concept of a natural sense of hearing; and to be reminded that the judgement of the intellect, according to the immutable rules or laws of number, was something that Augustine and his contemporaries found it impossible to relinquish.

When Augustine reaches what is effectively the summit of his ascent through the numbers of the soul's perception of rhythm and attains what he calls the 'judicial numbers' (*iudiciales*), by which it judges what has gone before, he is clearly aware that this ability to judge is, in reality, very much dependent on the earlier stages and, in particular, on the stage of memory or memorial numbers (*recordabiles*). This is because it is the memory which stores the sounds which the soul has perceived, so that they can be recognized as present to the mind, and which also makes it possible for them to be subsequently recollected by it (*et talis cognitio recognitio est et recordatio*).[103] Only then, finally, on the basis of recollection, can they be rationally evaluated and judged.[104]

---

[102]*mus.* 6.9.24.
[103]6.8.21.
[104]6.8.21–22.

Memory, then, has a crucial role to play, not least because it alone can provide a presence of things past, so to speak. As Augustine observes, in terms which closely foreshadow his more well-known treatment of time in *Confessions* 11,[105] 'unless memory helps us when we hear even the shortest syllable, so that the motion, which was created when the beginning sounded, remains in our mind, during that moment of time, when no longer the beginning but the end of the syllable is sounding, we cannot say that we have heard anything' (6.8.21).

Having duly acknowledged the importance of sense perception and memory, however, the Master and his pupil press on to establish how they must be judged. 'Judicial' numbers follow after 'sensuous' numbers (or the natural sense of hearing) and evaluate them according to the eternal and immutable rules of number. This opening section of book 6, which is concerned with how we hear, and above all, with how we apprehend what we hear, is then, to all intents and purposes, still firmly on classical ground: sensuous sound must give way to rational judgement.

An ontology of music

The firm ground begins to disconcertingly give way, however, and the landscape opens out into the fathomless heights and bottomless abysses of Christian theology, as soon as Augustine begins to discuss the where, how and why of what he has called judicial numbers – the final stage of musical perception. He clearly states that the eternal, immutable truths, according to which all perceptions of sound must be judged, belong to God: 'from where should we believe that the soul is given what is eternal and unchangeable, if not from the one, eternal, and unchangeable God'.[106]

Beyond the numbers/music perceived by the soul, which he has just analysed, then, is cosmic music, and without it the music apprehended by the soul would fall into dissonant disarray. It is not

---

[106]*mus.* 6.12.36.
[105]See Harrison (2010) on Confessions 11; Van Dusen (2014) 235–246 cites *conf.* 11.27.35 'it is not the things themselves, which no-longer are, that I measure, but something that remains infixed in my memory' (241).

only poetry or music which ultimately owe their existence and form to the eternal and immutable source of rhythm and harmony, but, as Ambrose's hymn makes clear, *all* created reality, from terrestrial things to celestial bodies. As Augustine observes, in a passage redolent of those in book 1 of his *De doctrina Christiana*, where he attempts to describe the proper attitude of the soul to that which is inferior to it, and to that which is above it, in terms of an order of love:

> Let us, therefore, not look askance at what is inferior to us, but let us place ourselves between what is below and what is above us, with the help of our God and Lord, in such a way that we are not offended by what is inferior but enjoy only what is superior .... But what is superior except that in which the highest, unshakeable, unchangeable, eternal equality (*aequalitas*) exists, where there is no time, because there is no change, and from which the times are created and set in order and modified in imitation of eternity, while the celestial rotation returns to the same place and recalls the celestial bodies to the same place and through the days and months and years and lustra and the other orbits of the stars obeys the laws of equality and unity and order (*legibus aequalitatis et unitatis et ordinationis obtemperat*)? In this way,

he adds, 'through the rhythmical succession of their times, the orbits unite the terrestrial things, subjected to the heavenly ones to the hymn of the universe (*carmini uniuersitatis*)'.[107]

What Augustine is alluding to in this rather extraordinary passage is the Pythagorean theory of cosmic harmony: that we apprehend the macrocosmic harmony of the spheres through the microcosmic harmonies we experience and encounter in created

---

[107]6.11.29 Cf *ep. 55.7.13; ep.* 166.13 on 'hymn of the universe'. On the sources of this idea in Plato, Pliny, Cicero, Plutarch, Nichomachus, Censorinus, Macrobius and Ptolomy, see Stone Davis (2011) 25–26 n. 53. Augustine's reflections on cosmic harmony very much resemble those of Gregory of Nyssa, in the prologue of his *Inscriptions of the Psalms* (Heine (ed.) (1997)). He argues that we are able to apprehend the silent, unhearable music of the spheres, just as we are able to apprehend the unknowable and ineffable God, in and through the delight occasioned by the microcosmic harmony of God's creation, of human beings, and most especially of singing, and that in this way the soul is healed and attains blessedness. Pickstock (1998) 9 relates this to a defence of polyphonic music: it accurately reflects the invisible, unhearable, fixed and unchanging, eternal movement of complex and multidimensional cosmic harmony.

reality.[108] His point is that this cosmic harmony – what he here calls 'equality' (*aequalitas*) – owes its existence to God, the *Deus Creator Omnium*, the Creator of All, and that it is through equality that we are able to apprehend Him, for He *is* perfect equality.

We should note that Augustine's allusion to cosmic harmony is relatively unusual; much more often we find him expressing these same insights in terms of Scripture: 'You have created all things in measure, number and weight' (Wisdom 11:20). This verse is one which he frequently reverts to across his works in order to describe the manner in which all created reality is the work of the Divine Creator; that it is drawn from nothing and made to exist by receiving form; and that this form consists of measure, number and weight. Augustine therefore asserts that measure, number and weight, which are found in God, before creation, are that by which He creates, so that all creatures resemble their Creator: they possess unity, goodness and beauty. Human beings, created in His image, are therefore able to return to Him, through the love which the manifestations of unity, order and beauty inspire.[109] This all no doubt sounds rather odd: the terms 'measure', 'number' and 'weight' are seemingly quantitative terms but, in fact, they have a qualitative significance and meaning. The point Augustine is making by means of this rather abstract terminology is a very concrete one: that whatever exists, exists because it possesses measure, number and weight; if these things are taken away, or if they are lost, then it falls back into nothingness. It is therefore a statement of the complete dependence of created reality upon the Creator of All, the *Deus Creator Omnium*. The use of these terms to rehearse this characteristically Augustinian argument is well illustrated – predictably enough – in his comments on a passage from a homily on the Prologue of John's Gospel: 'The one through

---

[108]6.11.29 Heninger (1974).

[109]In addition to Wisdom 11.21 (*omnia in mensura, numero et pondere disposuisti* e.g. *Gn adu. man.* 1.16.26) Augustine also used Eccles. 7.26 (*quaererem sapientiam et numerum* – e.g. *lib.arb.* 2.24). His most detailed treatment of the triad is found in *Gn litt.* 4.3.7–7.14. He often also uses the triad *modus, species, ordo* (e.g. *c. Faust.* 21.6; *Gn. litt.* 4.3.7). It would take more space than we have here to elaborate on these terms and their philosophical background. I have treated the subject in detail elsewhere: Harrison (1992) 101–112; Harrison (2006) 100–114; Balthasar (2006) 114–115; du Roy (1966); Jeserich (2013) 97–100 on philosophical background; Roche (1941) 350–376; Solignac *BA* 48 note complémentaire 18; Svoboda (1933).

whom the angel was made is the one through whom the maggot too was made ... Every single creature was made through Him, big and small; through Him were made the heights, through Him the depths; through him what is spiritual, through him what is bodily. There can be no shape, I mean, no organic structure, no harmony of parts, no substance of any sort that is able to have weight, number, measure, except through that Word from the Word, that is, the creator, to whom it is said "You have arranged all things in measure, and number and weight".'[110]

Augustine's understanding of music in terms of cosmic harmony, and of measure, number and weight, therefore provides the basis on which he elaborates what is a quite extraordinary theology of music in the concluding book of *De musica*: music, when understood in these terms, originates in God; it gives creation its existence and form; it gives human beings existence and form; they perceive creation and its Creator through music; they fall when they ignore or distort his music; they return to God when they hear, delight in and judge it correctly. Music, in other words, is that by which God creates, orders and redeems; it is of God, from God and returns us to God. Augustine sums up this theology of music towards the end of *De musica* when, returning to Ambrose's *Deus Creator Omnium*, he observes that all things, created from nothing, come from 'that supreme and eternal origin of rhythms and similarity and equality and order (*illo summo atque aeterno principatu numerorum et similitudinis et aequalitatis et ordinis*). But if you take these away from the earth, it will be nothing. Therefore God has created the earth, and it was created from nothing.'[111]

What Augustine is describing is no more and no less than an 'ontology' of music, and it is one that pushes him to insist that we cannot and must not remain at the instinctive level of the natural sense of hearing or 'sensuous numbers': it is not enough simply to remain at the level of intuitive delight; we need to be consciously aware that whatever delights us in temporal, mutable, sensuous music owes its existence to the eternal, immutable, transcendent God; that to fail to look in and through His admittedly beautiful creation would be to take creation for the Creator, to idolize it and to fail to worship its source. As we noted above, Augustine

---

[110]*tr. Jo.* 1.13.
[111]*mus.* 6.17.57 Cf *uera.rel.* 79.

expresses this conviction in the language of equality (*parilitas; aequalitas*). God, he insists, is the source of supreme equality – the source of that equal measure or music which so pleases us in sensible things.[112] We must, however, ensure that we do not take joy in things that merely imitate equality but do not yet achieve it, even though, as he comments, 'to the extent that they imitate equality, we cannot deny that they are beautiful in their own kind and order'. Rather, we must direct our joy to that supreme equality which they imitate.[113] In other words, as we have seen, Augustine urges that we must place ourselves between what is below us and what is above us so that 'we are not offended by what is inferior but only enjoy what is superior'.[114]

The effect of the Fall: Sensuous music and sensual concupiscence

We are no doubt used to these ideas in the Christian tradition, but it is difficult to know how to weigh them so that music – sensuous, sounded, performed music which delights the ear and affects the mind and soul – is not simply written off. It is all too easy to read Augustine, or any early Christian author, as doing precisely this. The basic problem, as far as they are concerned, is that we cannot rely on the soul's activity in sense perception or the natural sense of hearing we undeniably possess, not to be mistaken or deceived when we hear sensuous music. There are a number of reasons for this, and even as early as the *De musica*, Augustine is acutely conscious of them.

First of all, we must take account of the effect of the Fall[115] on the soul's relation to the body. It is clear to Augustine that, following the Fall, we cannot be confident that we will resist the seemingly

---

[112]*mus.* 6.10.26–29.
[113]6.11.28.
[114]6.11.29.
[115]Jeserich's ((2013) 72f) treatment of *De musica* is an example of a widespread scholarly tendency to fail to take what Augustine says about the Fall seriously and therefore to misinterpret him.

inevitable tendency to take what is heard as an end in itself, to seek to possess it, indeed to manipulate and dominate it, so that we fail to acknowledge its source, and the inherent contingency of it, and all created things, on God, their Creator.[116] He sums up the reason for the soul's fall as pride: in taking created reality as an end in itself and in attempting to subject it – and other rational souls – to itself, it has failed to acknowledge its Creator and its complete and utter dependence upon Him. In doing so it has fallen not just from the truth but from the source of its existence; it has literally diminished itself by self-destructive pride:

> The soul by itself is nothing – otherwise it would not be changeable and admit any decrease of its essence – so, since it is nothing by itself and whatever it has of existence comes from God, if it remains in its own place (*in ordine suo*), by God's own presence it is given life in its mind and conscience. ... Therefore, to be inflated by pride, this is for the soul to proceed to the extreme exterior and, as it were, to become empty (*inanescere*), which means to have less and less existence (*minus minusque esse*).[117]

It seems that the more the soul is obliged to attend to the body in sense perception the more it is distracted and diverted by it[118] – enfeebled, drawn down and dragged away from attention to eternal rhythms.[119] As Augustine observes, 'The soul dominates the now mortal and frail body with great difficulty and attention.'[120] This is because, following the Fall, the soul has become attached to the body rather than to God – a servant rather than a master.[121] In this state, each stage of sense perception, which we saw Augustine carefully analysing as part of the soul's ascent to judgement, effectively becomes something that waylays it: it is diverted by occurring rhythms, made restless by progressing rhythms, distracted by the

---

[116] 6.13.41 – the soul wishes to subject, rule and act upon other rational souls but cannot even rule itself now that it has turned away from contemplation of God.
[117] 6.13.40.
[118] 6.13.37.
[119] 6.5.12.
[120] 6.5.14.
[121] 6.5.13.

images and phantasms[122] produced in memorial rhythms; 'finally', Augustine observes, 'it is distracted by the love of the utterly vain thought of such things, and this it produces through sensual rhythms (*sensualibus numeris*), in which there is some kind of rules of an art which find a joy in imitation (*quasi regulae quaedam artis imitatione gaudentes*); out of these is born curiosity'.[123]

Thus, rather than allowing the soul to ascend to eternal and immutable rules of judgement, the perception of performed music becomes something that mires it in a deeper and deeper pit, until, entirely debilitated, it is surrounded only by the spectres of sensuous imitations. Even if it can momentarily glimpse the truth, it is wholly incapable of holding it fast[124]: 'being entangled in all these great distractions, is there any wonder if the soul is distracted from the contemplation of the truth? And to the extent that it pauses from these distractions, it sees the truth, but, since it has not yet overcome them, it is not allowed to remain in it.'[125]

Secondly, Augustine reflects that we cannot rely on the soul's activity in sense perception, or the natural sense of hearing, because, having turned away from its Creator and the eternal, immutable laws of truth, to the temporal, mutable, physical order, the soul now finds itself a part of that order – sewn into it, as it were – so that, like a statue in the corner of a beautiful building, a solider in the front line, or a syllable in a poem, it can only see in part, from its own now very limited perspective;[126] the beauty of Divine Providence now seems 'disordered and perturbed'[127] to it, and it

---

[122]6.11.32 – 'Thus, whatever this memory retains from the movements of the mind, which have been activated towards the reactions of the body, are called *phantasiai* in Greek, and I can find no better term in Latin.' To consider them as known and certain, however, is 'on the very threshold of error' and can lead to the formation of *phantasmata* – images of images, which are even further removed from certain knowledge.

[123]6.13.39.

[124]Augustine is slightly more optimistic in *ord.* 2.16.44 but still admits the difficulties which the soul faces when it turns within, away from the traces and vestiges of number in the senses to number itself. He notes that although it is often confronted by false images, it is possible for it to resist these images and press on to contemplation of divine things 'not just as truths to be believed, but as matters to be contemplated, understood and retained'.

[125]6.13.42 Cf *ord.* 2.15.43.

[126]*mus.* 6.9.30 Cf. *ord.* 2.19.51. This is closely related to Augustine's appraisal of the authority of the ancients, custom and tradition in 1–5.

[127]*mus.* 6.9.30.

is no longer able to appreciate the unity, harmony and equality of God's equal music.

Thirdly, what limited perception of music the fallen soul does have can tend to hinder and entrap it, rather than point it towards the whole. Music is undeniably beautiful: it occasions pleasure, delight and love, but unless they are rightly directed, they can simply become what Augustine describes as 'carnal lust' (*carnalem uoluptatem*),[128] an 'intimacy of the soul with the flesh (*animae consuetudo facta cum carne*)' which vitiates the soul, creating in it a struggle which renders it blind to the eternal music of God and powerless to order itself in accordance with it.[129]

So, music as sound, perceived by the activity of the soul in sense perception, is fraught with difficulties in a theological context. Is there a way out of this? Well, that is obviously the big question, and it is clear it relates not just to the performance of music but to all our interactions with the world as created beings.

An ethics and aesthetics of music

Having set out this daunting portrait of fallen human beings and the highly ambivalent role played by sound and sense perception in their fallen-ness, Augustine once again changes key in book 6. He has carefully analysed what we might call the psychology and ontology of music and, in the course of this analysis, has made a good deal of human failings and fallen-ness. Towards the end of book 6, however, he returns to sensuous music – to music as sound, judged by a natural sense of hearing – and reconsiders it in what we might call an ethical context. In doing so, I think he begins to hold out the possibility that the soul might be able to undertake its role in sense perception without being irretrievably dragged down by the 'sensuous concupiscence of the flesh'; that it might hear and, in the activity of hearing, move in and through what is heard towards what he has described as 'that supreme and eternal origin of rhythms and similarity and equality and order';[130] that the very

---

[128]6.15.45.
[129]6.11.33.
[130]*mus.* 6.16.45.

delights and pleasures afforded by the natural sense of hearing can be turned to good effect.[131]

The psychology and ontology of music he has already rehearsed give him good grounds for holding out this possibility. At the level of the soul, or psychology, all sound, insofar as it is rhythmical and harmonious – in other words, insofar as it can be perceived by the natural sense of hearing as pleasing and delightful and therefore as music rather than noise – owes its existence ultimately to God, the 'supreme and eternal origin of rhythms and similarity and equality and order (*summo atque aeterno principatu numerorum et similitudinis et aequalitatis et ordinis*)'.[132] At an ontological level, nothing would exist without the Creator bringing it into existence from nothingness. What delights and pleases the senses, and is judged as such by the natural sense of hearing, is not therefore bad, evil or to be rejected: it is not 'evil in itself'; rather, it is the good work of a good Creator. As Augustine comments: 'What soils the soul is not something evil, for even the body is a creation of God and is adorned by its own form, however low ... it is not the rhythms (*numeri*), which are inferior to reason and beautiful in their own kind, but the love of inferior beauty that soils the soul.'[133] Of musical rhythms themselves, he asserts that 'to the extent that they imitate equality we cannot deny that they are beautiful in their own kind and order'.[134]

Most importantly, he insists that even human sinfulness is not allowed to disrupt the beauty of the created order, but is, rather, comprehended by the order of God's providence; the beauty of the hymn of the universe is not allowed to falter.[135] He observes:

Let us remember – which is very relevant to our present discussion – that this [the purification and ordering of the fallen soul in this life] is done through the providence of God, through which he has created all things and rules over them, so that even the sinful and burdened soul should be activated by rhythms and

---

[131]There is a long tradition of Greek philosophical reflection on music which understands it as having an important influence in education, in moulding character, ordering the soul and on ethical behaviour. See Barker (1984) for texts.

[132]6.17.57.

[133]6.14.46 Cf 6.4.7.

[134]6.10.28.

[135]6.11.29–30.

activate rhythms until the final corruption of the flesh, which rhythms can certainly become less and less beautiful but not lack beauty altogether. But the supremely good and supremely just God does not look askance at any beauty, which is created either as a consequence of damnation or the returning and remaining of the soul. But the rhythm both begins from the one and is beautiful through equality and similarity and is united in order (*Numerus autem et ab uno incipit et aequalitate ac similitudine pulcher est et ordine copulatur*).[136]

Augustine has the same to say about the fallen body: although it has been 'changed for the worse by the first sin' and is now 'subject to death and corruption', nevertheless he insists that it has 'a beauty of its own kind and by that very fact it commends adequately the excellence of the soul, of which not even the wound and illness deserved to be without the honour of some distinction (*alicuius decoris*)' (6.4.7). The fitting distinction, of course, is God's providence and, in particular, the incarnation of Christ, 'God's highest Wisdom [who] deigned to take upon himself this wound through a wonderful and ineffable mystery when he became man without sin but not without the condition of the sinner, so that through his unmerited death in the body he atoned for our sinfulness' (6.4.7).[137] Like creation, therefore, however distorted and disfigured by sin the body is, it retains vestiges of order and beauty and is never without the saving grace of God's providence and incarnation.

Thus, Augustine sets forth an aesthetic of creation and providence in which everything that is created from nothing is beautiful insofar as it possesses form, and in which God's providential ordering of human sin, and most especially, his providential incarnation and redemption of sinful human beings, ensures that, despite sin, the beautiful order or hymn of the universe is preserved. Interestingly, he seems to be edging towards an aesthetic in which the very dissonance, ugliness and disfigurement brought about by sin can have a role in moving the perceiver towards harmony, beauty and

---

[136] 6.17.56 (Cf. 6.11.30). Cf *nat. boni* 36–38; *uera rel.* 44–45; *lib. arb.* 3.26–7. Augustine continued to compare the action and order of God's providence to music, e.g. *conf.* 9.6.14; *ep.* 166.13.

[137] *b. uita* 32–34; *uera.rel.* 57–58.

order. The former are represented as antitheses, or as parts, which gesture towards the whole[138] – ideas he will develop more fully later on, notably in reference to the beauty of the crucified Christ.[139]

What is at issue, then, is not the goodness and beauty of creation, of sensuous music, or even of the fallen body but a right use of them. As we have observed, it is striking just how much this section of *De musica* anticipates the first book of Augustine's later *De doctrina Christiana* (396–426/7). In the early work he attempts to set out the soul's position and role in relation to temporal rhythms in the same way as he considers its relation to created reality in the later work. In both works he does this in terms of a distinction between what the soul should rightfully use (*uti*) towards blessedness and what it should rightfully enjoy (*frui*) as an end in itself; in other words, between its use of created, temporal rhythms/reality and its enjoyment of the eternal, immutable God, who is their Creator and orderer. Foreshadowing what he will later say about the cross of Christ as a plank to which fallen human beings must cling, in order to cross the tumultuous sea of the world,[140] he comments that

> whatever rhythms have been produced by the mortality that we have received as punishment, let us not deny that they are a creation of divine providence, as they are beautiful in their own kind, but let us not love them, as if we would be blessed by enjoying such rhythms. For since they are temporal, we will be rid of these rhythms, as of a plank in the waves, not by throwing them away as a burden, nor by embracing them as something well anchored, but by using them well.[141]

The distinction between use and enjoyment is not quite as straightforward as it might first appear, however, and it is in this context that Augustine introduces a further element, alongside use and enjoyment, which will prove to be of the utmost significance for his theology in general, as well as for his theology of music: it

---

[138]Cf *nat. boni* 13–18; *ord* 1.1.2; 1.7.18; 2.4.13; 2.19.51; *uera rel.* 76; *ep.* 29.11; *ciu.* 11.18 and 23. In this context he sometimes uses the example of silences or rests in singing, which, although an absence or a lack, contribute to the beauty of the whole, e.g. *Gn.litt.imp.* 5.25.
[139]e.g. *s.* 27.6; *ep.Jo.* 9.9; *en.Ps.* 44.1; 95.4.
[140]*Jo.eu.tr.* 28.5.
[141]6.14.46 Cf 6.11.29. This is systematically developed in *doc. Chr.* 1.

is love, or more precisely, the double commandment of love of God and love of neighbour. 'The holy Scriptures', he writes,

> in so many volumes and with such authority and sanctity tell us nothing but this, that we shall love our God and Lord with all our heart and with all our soul and with all our mind and love our neighbour as ourselves. Thus, if we direct all these movements and rhythms (*motus numerosque*) of our human activity to this end we will undoubtedly be purified.[142]

Use therefore becomes a form of love, which, when directed towards our neighbour and towards our Creator, ensures that all the 'rhythms of our human activity',[143] in other words, our perceptions, actions, memories and judgements, are rightly ordered towards enjoyment of God, rather than falling into the snares of pride, the desire for domination, carnal lust or curiosity.[144] Thus, Augustine concludes, 'The soul maintains its order by loving with its whole self what is superior to it, that is to say God, but its fellow souls as itself. For by this virtue of love the soul adorns everything that is inferior to it but is not soiled by what is inferior.'[145] The soul's order is therefore an order of love.

What Augustine describes as an attitude of use rather than enjoyment, therefore, is not so much an attitude which derives from an intellectual understanding of the nature of reality, or a rational judgement according to the eternal and immutable rules of rhythm and harmony, but is first and foremost an attitude of love – of rightly ordered love. For the first time, I think, he here articulates an idea which is to be one of the structuring principles of his theology: that 'our weight is our love'; that we are drawn towards things because we love them; that it is love which orders our affections; and, above all, that this love is inspired by the fact that something delights us: if something does not occasion delight then it does not motivate us or inspire us to seek out its source and its fullness.[146] As we have seen, he writes:

---

[142]6.14.43.
[143]6.14.43.
[144]6.14.45.
[145]6.14.46.
[146]It is interesting to note that Augustine expounds these ideas well before *Simpl.* 2.21 (396), where most Augustine scholars usually locate their first appearance. Cf *conf.* 13.9.10; *ciu.* 11.28; *ep.* 55.10.18; 207.2.9.

Let us, therefore, not look askance at what is inferior to us, but let us place ourselves between what is below us and what is above us, with the help of our God and Lord, in such a way that we are not offended by what is inferior but enjoy only what is superior. [He then adds] For the pleasure is like a weight for the soul (*Delectatio quippe quasi pondus est animae*). And so pleasure sets the soul in its place. 'For where your treasure is, there will your heart be also', where your pleasure is, there will your treasure be, but where your heart is, there your beatitude or misery will be. (6.11.29)

The pleasure and love inspired by beautiful, sensuous rhythm, then, draw us to its source and end: the eternal, immutable, equal music of God. This is because, as we have seen, what inspires love in sensuous rhythms – equality, similarity and order – is ontologically continuous with the eternal Creator, orderer and redeemer. In making this point Augustine stops just short of identifying God with love and love as an ontological category (though this identification is clearly implicit):

Rhythm both begins from the one and is beautiful through equality and similarity and is united in order ... therefore all things, inasmuch as they exist, have been made and created from one origin through a form, equal and similar to this origin by the richness of its goodness, through which they are united with each other as one, and as one from the one, by the loveliest love, so to speak.[147]

Augustine is therefore insistent that, while we perform temporal rhythms, we must focus on immortal and changeless ones and that the very act of performing them inculcates the virtues which make this possible: listening to temporal rhythms we anticipate the joys of eternal ones, and in this anticipation the virtues of temperance, fortitude, justice and prudence are inculcated and exercised.[148] Indeed, he seems to want to argue for a state in which our engagement with temporal rhythms becomes almost unconscious – a state in which they do not distract or waylay us, because the soul is not focused on

---

[147]6.17.56 Jacobsson's translation is inspired. The Latin reads: '*qua inter se unum et de uno unum carissima, ut ita dicam, caritate iunguntur, omnia facta esse atque condita quaecumque sunt, in quantumcumque sunt*'.
[148]6. 15.49.

them but on their eternal source. Sensuous rhythms might indeed lead the fallen soul back to this source, but for the one who has been purified, they become unconscious, instinctive actions: we walk, dance and sing spontaneously and intuitively. 'But if', he comments,

> when we think with utmost attention of things that are incorporeal and always the same, we at that same moment happen to activate some temporal rhythms (*numeros temporales*) in some easy and completely normal movement of the body, either while walking or singing (*psallentes*) [the temporal rhythms] pass away without our noticing them at all, even though they would not exist unless we were activating them. And finally, if they pass away in the same way when we are occupied with our futile *phantasmata* [*inanibus phantasmatis* – images impressed on the mind by the soul as a result of sense perception] so that we activate them without perceiving them, how much more and how much more persistently, 'when this corruptible has put on incorruption, and this mortal has put on immortality'.[149]

Of course, what Augustine is describing here is an ideal state – one that will only be achieved in the life to come. Interestingly, he is also describing our original, unfallen state – the state of Adam and Eve in paradise, unaware of being naked, unselfconscious, directly and intuitively aware of divine wisdom, engaging in sexual intercourse without any of the disturbing concupiscence which characterizes it after the Fall.[150] Just as a craftsman undertakes his work with intuitive, unselfconscious skill; just as we move our hands and feet to perform their special functions without conscious effort; just as Adam and Eve would have engaged in sexual intercourse in intuitive obedience to a will undisturbed by lust before the Fall,[151] so, in an ideal state, we might listen to, or perform, sensuous music and remain undistracted by its temporal rhythms, from its eternal and immutable source. As we will see in Chapter 3, Augustine is here anticipating what he will say about wordless jubilation or joyful

---

[149]6.15.49.
[150]*ciu.* 14.23 on sexual intercourse before the Fall; Cf *doc. Chr.* 2.34.52–37.55 where Augustine is discussing the truths of the liberal arts. These are not 'instituted by men; rather [they are] ... discovered in the order of things' (2.35.53). Their order is not primarily one we need to rationally apprehend but one we must observe.
[151]*ciu.* 14.23.

singing, which springs spontaneously and unselfconsciously from the heart and unites the singer with God, so that they 'enter into the joy of the Lord'.

Thus, hearing music so that it simply resonates directly, instinctively and intuitively, with an uninterrupted participation in eternal, equal music – becoming the music while the music lasts – is the joy that awaits us in the life to come. In this life, however, Augustine is clear that we need to notice and feel the music of temporal, mutable, earthly rhythms and have our natural sense of hearing engaged by sensuous music, for only then can fallen human beings be drawn, in and through the love it inspires, to delight in its eternal source. Our natural and spontaneous delight in sensuous music is thus a foreshadowing of the spontaneous, undistracted joy in eternal and equal music, which will be ours in the life to come.

Anticipating what we will find in Confessions 9 and the ascent at Ostia (which we will discuss in the next chapter), Augustine therefore asks in *De musica*, 'What activity is prescribed for it [the soul] by God, by which it is purified and unburdened and may fly back to the quiet and enter into the joy of its Lord?' (a direct reference to the ascent at Ostia, if ever there was one). The answer, as we have seen, is the double commandment: 'Scripture tells us nothing but this .... If we direct all these movements and rhythms of our human activity to this end we will undoubtedly be purified.'[152]

The conversion of the senses

Augustine summarizes the destructive lusts (*carnalem uoluptatem*) that so beset the soul's perception of sensuous music in reference to 1John 2.16: 'the lust of the flesh, the lust of the eyes and the pride of life'.[153] Having done so, he revisits each of the rhythms of perception he has set out and defined so carefully earlier on in *De musica* and demonstrates how they can, in fact, be converted, from

---

[152]6.14.43.
[153]6.14.44–15.45 This is a text which he often uses in this context.

carnal lust and proud, possessive domination, towards the health of
the soul, by love of God and neighbour. He observes that, the one

> who directs all these rhythms which belong to the body and exist
> towards the reactions of the body (*aduersus passiones corporis*),
> and those among the rhythms that are contained in the memory,
> not to carnal lust (*carnalem uoluptatem*) but solely for his bodily
> health ... and who refers all those rhythms that are active upon
> the souls that are joined to his soul or that are exerted in order
> to join such souls to it, and who refers those rhythms among
> those that stay in memory not to his own proud superiority but
> to their usefulness for the souls themselves, and who uses those
> rhythms well [sensuous rhythms], which in the case of both
> kinds [for bodily health or for one's neighbour] preside in the
> sense as some kind of rulers and investigators (*quasi moderatores
> exploratoresque*) over the others that pass away, not for the
> purpose of a superfluous and dangerous curiosity but for the
> purpose of a necessary approval or disapproval? Does he not
> activate all those rhythms without being trapped in any of their
> snares. For he both chooses the health of the body, so as not to
> be hindered, and refers all those activities to usefulness for his
> neighbour, whom he is commanded to love as himself because
> of the natural bond of a universal law (*communis iuris naturale
> uinculum*).[154]

We find the same process set out in *De ordine*, which, as we
have noted, was written just before the *De musica* and in many
respects foreshadows it. In this work, Augustine draws together the
ideas we have been exploring when he makes a distinction between
delight of the senses and delight *through* the senses – between the
delight of the senses inspired by the sweetness of song, and delight
through the senses in the song's meaning or rational, rhythmic
measure. The distinction is one between metre and meaning, sound
and signification, sweet song and the 'divine and eternal' rules of

---

[154] 6.14.45 This will only be fully achieved in the life to come, when the soul will
be turned to God and will 'give the music of health (*numeros sanitatis*) to the body
without receiving any [misdirected] joy from it' (6.11.33; Cf 6.15.49).

number.[155] It is important to note that these are not separated out but that the movement from sense to meaning is effected precisely by delight in the sweetness of song heard by the ears, *through* which it is led to delight in its meaning or truth. He comments, 'Who, indeed, does not see that in songs (*carminibus*) – and we likewise say that in them there is a sweetness that pertains to the ears (*uoluptatem aurium*) – rhythm(*dimensionem*) is the producer of this sweetness?'[156]

Augustine first gives the example of the rhythmical art of dance: 'the dance itself is called *reasonable* (*rationabilis*), because it aptly signifies and exhibits something over and above the delight of the senses ... The eyes would be offended if the movements were not graceful, for that pertains to sense, in which the soul perceives delight precisely because it is united with the body.' He then makes the same point in relation to music:

> Therefore, delight of the sense is one thing; delight *through* the sense is something else (*Aliud ergo sensus, aliud per sensum*). Graceful movement delights the sense, but the timely import of the movement delights the mind alone *through* the sense (*per sensum*). This is more easily noticed in hearing: whatever has a pleasing sound (*jocunde sonat*), that it is which pleases and entices the hearing itself. What is really signified by that sound is what is borne to the mind though the messenger of our hearing ... our praise of the metre is one thing, but our praise of the meaning is something else (*Aliter metra laudamus, aliterque sententiam*).[157]

However, as we noted at the beginning of this chapter, the question of just *how* we apprehend the 'meaning' is to a certain extent left hanging in *De ordine*. Is it through a natural sense of hearing or through reasoned judgement, or both? In other words, is it a matter of pleasure and delight or of reason? The related question

---

[155]*ord.* 2.14.41 Cf *doc. Chr.* 2.3.4 – the trumpet, flute and harp make sounds which are not only pleasing but also significant.

[156]*ord.* 2.11.34.

[157]Ibid. This passage is followed by an extended demonstration of this process, as Augustine proceeds to describe an ascent through the disciplines of the liberal arts: from the 'shadows and vestiges of reason' in the senses to ultimate truth and wisdom in God (2.15.42).

of whether the soul is aware of the immutable and eternal rules by which it must judge, or whether, following the Fall, it is aware only of what has been brought to it by its activity in sense perception, is also one that remains unclear. The reader will recollect that at the very beginning of *De musica*, sense, memory and imitation were contrasted with reason and identified as that which we share with the beasts. Augustine writes:

> M 'Do you attribute the sense of hearing to the mind, to the body or to both?'; D 'to both'; M 'and memory?'; D 'To the mind, I think. For if we perceive by the senses something we commit to memory that is no reason to think we must consider memory to be in the body'; M. 'This happens to be a great question, and one not proper to this discussion.'[158]

In attempting to establish what Augustine's answer to this 'great question' actually is, scholars appear to be divided as to whether he thinks we actually need to hear music for the mind to be aware of it or whether we already apprehend the eternal and immutable archetype of music within. Do we need sensuous sound and sensuous perception, or do we possess a silent, eternal and immutable music within, which sensuous music can at best remind us of, and by which it must be judged? Is it the case that what comes to us through the senses is merely an inferior imitation of the archetype of eternal and immutable music which we already possess within, which must therefore be judged and set aside? As we have seen, the great Augustine scholar and music critic, Henri Irenée Marrou, takes this to be self-evident.[159] But on the basis of what we have discovered in book 6 of *De musica*, in the course of attending to Augustine's theological reflection on music, it does indeed appear that without sensuous music; without performed music; without what Augustine, in the following passage, calls 'more lively rhythms (*numeris uiuacioribus*)', we cannot begin to apprehend the eternal, immutable music which gives it existence and form. Having defined the levels of the soul's perception of music, and considering the relation between sensuous numbers and judicial numbers, he writes:

---

[158]Ibid. 1.4.8.
[159]Writing under the pseudonym Henri Davenson (1942) e.g. 23–30.

If we were right in thinking that unless the sense of pleasure itself were imbued with some rhythms, it would never have been able to approve of equal intervals and reject confused ones, then we are also right in thinking that reason (*ratio*), which is placed above this pleasure, cannot in any way judge the rhythms that it possesses below itself, without some more lively rhythms (*numeris uiuacioribus*).[160]

I would suggest that sensuous music is needed for two reasons: it is not just because we are now fallen, and have lost an inward, intuitive apprehension of eternal music, but first and foremost, as Ambrose's *Deus Creator Omnium* reminds Augustine, because we are created; because we ourselves owe our existence and form to God, the Creator of All, who will always transcend us.

In other words, as I suggested at the beginning of this chapter, I think that what we find in the *De musica* is a significant departure from a classical, Platonic understanding of perception towards a Christian, theological understanding which, as we have seen, takes full account of our creation from nothing by God the Creator of All; of the Fall; of our inability to know or to judge eternal and immutable music; and of our dependence upon God's gracious creative, providential and redeeming activity – all of which takes place precisely in and through our encounter with His temporal, mutable music. The memory, by which the soul comprehends this activity – remembering and recollecting it when it has passed, being aware of it in the present, and stretching out towards its source in the life to come – is therefore essential, not so much as the source of rational judgement according to immutable rules but as the source of our encounter with the temporal, mutable, sensuous music which alone conveys them to us.[161] It is only in hearing, recollecting, attending to, and above all, delighting in and loving music that we are able to apprehend it. Music may well be rational, but we only apprehend it because it is rhythmically ordered, and these rhythms

---

[160]*mus.* 6.9.24.
[161]Cf *trin.* 11.3.9–4.18; 14.3.13–4.16 – on how memory is essential for the mind to remember, understand and love itself and above all, to remember, understand and love God, from whom, through whom and in whom are all things (Rom. 11.36 – *trin.* 14.4.16). The same process is described in *conf.* 11 in relation to hearing and it is significant that Augustine's example here is again Ambrose's *Deus Creator Omnium*. See Harrison (2010).

can only be apprehended in time, by means of sense perception, retained and recollected in the memory.[162]

Sensuous rhythms revisited

In conclusion, then, I would like to suggest that the very Augustinian doctrine of love, set out in *De musica* in response to his disturbing portrait of fallen humanity, is no more and no less than a theological re-articulation of the 'natural sense of hearing' which we have seen intuitively judges music on the basis of whether it is pleasing or offensive. This theological restatement of the natural sense of hearing is one which opens up the possibility of allowing a much more positive role for music experienced as delightful sound than Augustine's unsparing analysis of the effects of the Fall seemed to allow earlier on in book 6. Of course, this is because a theology of music comprehends not only creation and the Fall but also grace, which providentially orders created, temporal reality and sinful human beings so that their beauty is retained; they continue to inspire love and delight and thereby become the means in and through which the Creator draws his creation back to Himself. In *De musica*, it is through sensuous rhythm – through a natural, intuitive sense of delight and pleasure in hearing God's music played out in creation, providence and redemption – as well as hymns, poetry, dance and song – that grace works in order to heal the soul and return it to the divine.

At the end of book 6 Augustine returns to the *Deus Creator Omnium*.[163] Voicing and hearing it again he is aware of the way it has operated on his thought at a number of different levels: it is a correct and pleasing line of poetry, like the many other lines of

---

[162]Cf *mus.* 6.8.21 'And those occurring rhythms which are surely not produced according to their own will, but according to the reactions of the body, are presented to the judicial rhythms for judgment and are judged by them to the extent that the memory is able to retain their intervals. For this kind of rhythm consists of temporal intervals, and unless we are assisted by memory in this, it cannot in any way be judged by us.' As Court (1987) 177, succinctly puts it: 'Without memory of number, there is no time and without time, there is no poetry or music.' Cf Van Dusen (2014) 211–220. It is this contrast which Augustine will later describe in terms of *sapientia* and *scientia* (*trin* 13).

[163]6.17.57.

classical verse he has analysed in the course of his treatise; it is music, rhythmically ordered and harmoniously pleasing, lending itself to sung performance; it is apprehended by the soul in sense perception, when it reverberates in the ears, and is stored, recollected and judged by the soul; it is a statement of the fundamental theological truth that every aspect of created reality – every plant, animal, element or particle – witnesses to the supreme, eternal music of the Creator, who has drawn them from nothing; above all, it brings together musical sound and meaning so that the sound, by inspiring love and delight, reorientates fallen human attention and brings it to the reality or meaning it so compellingly conveys.[164]

Despite the closing emphasis on love, the *De musica* may well strike the reader as a rather over-intellectualized consideration of music. Augustine is well aware that the approach he has taken in this treatise is simply a symptom of his own character: he is an intellectual – someone who needs to get their mind round things, to understand, define, categorize and prove things in order to satisfy his restless curiosity. He ends the work by admitting this and observing that those who are willing and able to believe and trust God's authority and Christian teaching, without the need for rational argument, are in a position to grasp the truths he has laboured over – and dragged his long-suffering and patient interlocutor and reader through – in a much more direct and (dare we say it?) natural or intuitive sense.[165] The contrast between reason and faith is one that runs throughout Augustine's works, but it is not so much a tension as a complementary relation: faith already 'knows' and loves what reason seeks to rationally demonstrate; faith practices what reason attempts to theorize; faith hears, delights in and loves what reason merely describes: the eternal and immutable music

---

[164]6.17.57–58.

[165]He makes the same observation in *ord.* 2.16.44–2.17.46: the way of the liberal arts is extremely difficult and only for 'some very gifted person who even from boyhood has constantly and earnestly applied himself'. He holds out the way of faith in the mysteries for those who have nothing to do with the liberal arts. Cf *doc. Chr* 2.37.55; *conf.* 4.16.30–31 where Augustine comments that he acquired the liberal arts easily but they were of no use to him because he didn't use them properly, in referring them to God rather than his own pride in his rational powers. In contrast, weaker, less intelligent people, did not wander from God: 'They did not forsake you, but stayed safely in the nest of your Church to grow their plumage and strengthen the wings of their charity on the wholesome nourishment of faith.'

of the *Deus Creator Omnium*. As Augustine comments in the concluding paragraph of the work, 'These things have been written for much weaker persons than those who, following the authority of the two testaments, venerate and worship the one supreme God's consubstantial and unchangeable Trinity, by believing, hoping and loving it, from whom everything, through whom everything, in whom everything exists. For they are purified not through the brilliance of human arguments but through the most powerful and burning fire of love.'[166]

---

[166]*mus*. 6.17.59 See Pickstock (1998) 15–16 'he [Augustine] resolves.... the question of how it is that the soul can search for, and later reactivate harmonies which it does not at present know, by appeal to the role of desire. Indeed, for Augustine, desire always accompanies judgement ... this co-belonging of desire and judgement is summed up for Augustine in the image of reason become the burning fire of charity' (*mus*. 6.17.59).

2

The Conversion
of the Affections

And when they'd put aside desire for food and drink,
the Muse inspired the bard
to sing the famous deeds of fighting heroes
the song whose fame had reached the skies those days:
The Strife Between Odysseus and Achilles, Peleus' Son ....
That was the song the famous harper sang
but Odysseus, clutching his flaring sea-blue cape
in both powerful hands, drew it over his head
and buried his handsome face,
ashamed his hosts might see him shedding tears.
Whenever the rapt bard would pause in the song,
He'd lift the cape from his head, wipe off the tears
And hoisting his double-handled cup, pour it out to the gods.
But soon as the bard would start again, impelled to sing
by Phaeacia's lords, who reveled in his tale,
again Odysseus hid his face and wept.
His weeping went unmarked by all the others;
only Alcinous, sitting close beside him,
noticed his guest's tears,
heard the groan in the man's labored breathing.
(Homer *Odyssey* 8. 85–90; 99–113) (Fagles (1996) 193–194)

Unmoved his mind: the tears roll down in vain
(*Aeneid* 4.449, quoted in *ciu.* 9.4)

We beseech Christ and the Father,
and the Spirit of Christ and the Father,
who are one and omnipotent.
O Trinity, assist us who pray to you!

Christum rogamus et Patrem,
Christi Patrisque Spiritum,
unum potens per omnia;
foue precantes, Trinitas
(Ambrose *Deus Creator Omnium* (Ramsay(1997) 170–171))

In book 6 of *De musica* we saw that Augustine began his account
of Christian music with an analysis of how we perceive it: how
we hear, record, remember and judge what is sung. He struggled
with the subject and so do Augustine scholars. What is it, in human
beings, that actually hears? He makes it clear that it is not the ears
themselves; they simply capture and convey what is heard to that
which does the hearing, recording, remembering and judging. But
what is this? Should we refer to the heart (*cor*), the soul (*anima*),
the mind (*mens*), memory (*memoria*), intellect (*intellectus*), will
(*uoluntas*) or love (*amor*)? Augustine doesn't help: he often seems
to use these terms synonymously, sometimes in the same passage.
When we follow his lead and turn to focus specifically on how we
hear not just words, but music, we encounter even more difficulties.
Discussion of the role of visual or verbal images, and of memory and
mimesis, in relation to how sense perception brings about cognition
and action, has received a lot of attention in recent scholarship, not
least in reference to rhetoric but also in the context of the study of
the memory,[1] sight,[2] smell,[3] listening[4] and in relation to what has
been called the 'corporeal imagination'.[5] But almost no attention
has been given to the perception of music, especially non-verbal
music, by scholars of early Christianity.

I suspect that the question of how we think about the perception
of music is part of the much wider question of how we think about

[1]Carruthers (1990).
[2]Frank (2000).
[3]Ashbrook Harvey (2006).
[4]Harrison (2013).
[5]Cox Miller (2009).

the role of the 'non-rational' senses – touch, taste and smell. Does the language of sense perception, memorial images, cognition and action really fit and, if so, how? Is music rational? What Augustine has to say when he contrasts the rational senses of sight and hearing with the non-rational senses of taste, touch and smell, in the *De ordine*, cogently highlights this dilemma: in a passage we encountered in the last chapter, he observes: 'With regard to the eyes, that is usually called beautiful in which the harmony of parts is wont to be called reasonable; with regard to the ears, when we say that a harmony (*concentum*) is reasonable and that a rhythmic poem (*cantumque numerosum*) is reasonably composed, we properly call it sweet' and continues,

> But, we are not wont to pronounce it reasonable when the color in beautiful objects allures us or when a vibrant chord sounds pure and liquid (*neque in aurium suauitate cum pulsa chorda quasi liquide sonat atque pure*), so to speak. We must therefore acknowledge that, in the pleasure of those senses, what pertains to reason is that in which there is a certain rhythmic measure (*ubi quaedam dimensio est atque modulatio*).[6]

But what – one is left wondering, rather wistfully – about that 'vibrant ... pure and liquid' chord? It might not be 'reasonable' but is it not also beautiful and sweet? How, then, is it to be heard, recorded, remembered and judged?

It is indeed difficult to think of the memorial images created by the perception of music as visual or even verbal, especially as the effect of music (like taste, touch and smell) is more often described in terms of affective cognition – in terms of emotion and feeling – than of intellectual cognition.[7] It is at this point that the theologian must admit to a disconcerting sense that the already uncertain ground beneath their academic feet is beginning to give way: there is a minor industry of work on the effect of music on the mind/brain by musicologists and psychologists which cannot but make a theologian feel rather naive. Moreover, having mentioned 'affective cognition' in contrast to 'intellectual cognition', it is not entirely

---

[6]*ord.* 2.11.33.
[7]For a systematic account of the images created by perception see *Gn. litt.* 12.23.49.

clear how they differ. The ancients would no doubt be immediately
suspicious and generally dismissive of such language: reason (*ratio*)
was responsible for any apprehension we might be able to attain
of truth, goodness and beauty – for any virtue we might be able
to achieve.[8] Certain 'good' or wise passions (*eupatheiai*; Latin:
constantiae) were indeed allowed – wishing, caution and joy – but
only so long as they were based on knowledge and judgement of
whether they are related to good or bad objects.[9] The majority of
the passions (*pathe*; Latin: *passiones, affectiones, perturbationes*),[10]
however, were held to be foolish, irrational emotions which were to
be studiously avoided as subversive, unsettling distractions which
undermined and frustrated reason. The ideal was to be free of
such emotions, and if you found that an emotion was beginning
to threaten, or were involuntarily subject to one (what the Stoics
called 'pre-passions' or 'first movements'), then it was necessary to
bring reason to bear: to decisively judge the emotion as good or
bad and either assent or dissent to it, before it became a full-blown
passion which would overwhelm reason. Only rational, voluntary,
deliberated, carefully judged emotions were held to be good, since
they ensured a freedom from irrational, involuntary, spontaneous
and uncontrollable passion. Indeed, the goal for the Stoics was
to be 'passionless', in other words, to achieve what they called
apatheia or freedom from the passions.[11] There were, of course,
exceptions to this way of thinking,[12] but the predominant tendency
in philosophical circles was to regard the emotional aspect of music
as a reason for sidelining it: it was written off as the expression
of irrational emotion – as something which cannot be subjected
to appraisal or judgement, something which at best inspires good,
ennobling feelings which can form character and lead to ethical
actions but which more often simply distracts or undermines the
will and reason or, worse, gives rise to undesirable passions which

---

[8]Sorabji (2000).

[9]*ciu.* 14.8.

[10]Brachtendorf (1997) for a very useful account of the understanding of the passions
in Cicero and Augustine.

[11]For Augustine's rejection of Stoic *apatheia* see *ciu.* 9.4; 14.9–10.

[12]Notably the widely accepted doctrine of the *eupatheiai*; Aristotle's teaching that
most emotions are useful in moderation (*metriopatheia*) – Sorabji (2000) 194f; and
Poseidonius's (135–51BC) more positive consideration of the role of non-rational
emotion in music – Sorabji (2000) 94–132.

can lead to sinful actions.[13] No one, not even classical philosophers or early Christian theologians, seems to have questioned the inherent power of music to impress the soul, to move it, and even to calm, heal, purify and strengthen it; the problem, as we have just glimpsed in the last chapter, was how to get a hold on it so that those formidable powers are harnessed to the good.

In this chapter, I'd like to try to get a hold on music in an early Christian context by examining one of the texts in which Augustine, in a number of now well-known episodes, admits to being moved by music and acknowledges its power. The text I have in mind is *Confessions* book 9. I'd like to suggest three things: that following Augustine's account of the conversion of his intellect and his will in books 1–8 of the *Confessions*, book 9 could well be described as an account of the conversion of his affections; secondly, that this conversion of the affections is directly related to his encounter with the music he heard in Milan following his conversion; and thirdly, that in each of the episodes in which music appears in book 9 we can identify a common pattern, which allows us to begin to describe how musical perception works to bring about what I have called affective cognition and which decisively breaks with the classical tradition of reflection on the passions which we have briefly outlined above. The first few stages of this pattern are ones we are now familiar with from our reading of the *De musica*: in each of the passages we will examine in *Confessions* book 9, music is played or sung, it resonates in the ears, is perceived by the soul, impressed by the soul upon the mind/memory, and leads to affective cognition. We have already seen this pattern of musical perception meticulously set out in the *De musica*, where we noted the key role which Augustine assigns to the penultimate level of perception or what he calls 'sensuous rhythms' (the 'natural sense of hearing'). These rhythms, we suggested, were identified by Augustine as the means by which God's grace works to inspire in the fallen soul – which is no longer able to judge by reason – a love and delight in the good, summed up in the double commandment of love of God and neighbour.

---

[13]Sorabji (2000) provides an account of the various philosophical approaches. See also Braund and Gill (1997); Clark (2016); Fitzgerald (2008); Graver (2007); Kaster (2005); Nussbaum (1994) on the emotions/passions in antiquity. I cannot agree with those scholars (e.g. Byers (2013)) who insist that Augustine remained faithful to this Stoic tradition of rational judgement.

Later on, in the context of his reflections on the Trinitarian operation of grace, and his attempts to describe how we come to participate in the divine Trinity through our encounter with God's temporal revelation, Augustine uses the terms 'memory', 'understanding' and 'will'/'love' (*memoria, intellectus, voluntas/ amor*) of the three components of the human mind, which work inseparably to bring human beings not only to affective or intellectual cognition but to God; since it is in the memory, understanding and will that we are formed and reformed in His image.[14] I think that these terms should also help us to describe the way in which our perception of music works to form, reform and conform the soul to God. In the later books of *De trinitate* Augustine makes it clear that as fallen creatures, we are entirely dependent on what we perceive through the senses for what we remember, understand and will/ love; that it is only through sense perception that we are led to spiritual perception; that what the memory contains and what we become aware of through recognition and recollection is based, first and foremost, on our perception of God's revelation of Himself to us through temporal, corporeal mediators: through creation, providence, the Scriptures and above all, the Incarnate Son. In this respect, 'understanding' in fallen human beings comprehends not so much rational cognition as affective cognition (in faith, hope and love), and 'will' comprehends not so much rationally deliberated free choice as the direction or movement (*intentio*) of the will in love.

In addition to what we have already discovered of the effects of the fallen soul's lust and pride in *De musica*, then, I would like to briefly note a number of salient points in Augustine's description of the image of God in the *De trinitate*, which will hopefully enable us to appreciate more fully his earlier reflection on these matters, in relation to music.

Firstly, in *De trinitate*, Augustine insists that it is not in remembering, understanding and loving ourselves that we are in the image of God but in remembering, understanding and loving the Divine Trinity, who is the source of our existence and is always present to us:

---

[14]E.g. *trin.* 15.22.42. For a detailed account of Augustine on the Trinity, see Ayres (2010); Gioia (2008).

This trinity of the mind is not really the image of God because the mind remembers and understands and loves itself, but because it is also able to remember and understand and love Him by whom it was made. And when it does this it becomes wise ... It is man's great misfortune not to be with Him without whom he cannot be. Obviously he is not without Him in whom he is; and yet if he fails to remember and understand and love Him, he is not with Him.[15]

Secondly, what Augustine calls 'understanding' (*intellegentia*) in this context arises primarily from a perception of created, sensuous reality, which, once impressed upon the mind and memory as a mental image, is cognized by faith and love. In other words it derives from what he calls knowledge, or *scientia*,[16] as opposed to the direct, inward illumination of divine Wisdom which human beings enjoyed before the Fall (*sapientia*).

Furthermore, the *De trinitate* makes it clear that it is only in and through Christ, who is both fully man and fully God, temporal and eternal, that the image of God in which we were created – our memory, understanding and love – is able to be reformed. This is brought about in and through the faith, hope and love which the incarnate Christ inspires to participate once again in the life of the Divine Trinity:

Our knowledge therefore is Christ, and our wisdom is the same Christ (*Scientia ergo nostra Christus est, sapientia quoque nostra idem Christus est*). It is he who plants faith in us about temporal things, he who presents us with the truth about eternal things. Through him we go straight toward him, through knowledge toward wisdom (*per scientiam ad sapientiam*), without ever turning aside from one and the same Christ 'in whom are hidden all the treasures of wisdom and knowledge'. (Col. 2:3)[17]

Finally, the *De trinitate* explains that 'will' (*uoluntas*), which before the Fall was the freedom to choose, is now the work of the Holy Spirit inspiring love and delight in what comes to the mind

---

[15]*trin.* 14.4.15–16.
[16]*trin.* 13.18.24; 14.1.3.
[17]*trin.* 13.19.24.

through the senses so that our memory, understanding and love might be converted towards God, who *is* love and the source of the love by which we love Him: "What have you that you have not received? And if you have received it, why do you boast as if you had not received it?' But when the mind truly recalls its Lord after receiving his Spirit, it perceives quite simply – for it learns this by a wholly intimate instruction from within – that it cannot rise except by his gracious doing, and that it could not have fallen except by its own willful undoing'.[18]

In the light of what we have briefly established concerning Augustine's theology of the image in *De trinitate*, I would therefore like to argue that the affective cognition[19] which arises from listening to music is essentially based on an awareness of the images impressed upon the mind through sense perception, which it cognizes through memory, understanding and will, and that broadly speaking, this process is the same operation that we have seen Augustine describe in terms of the natural sense of hearing in *De musica*.

In *Confessions* book 10, in the course of his examination of the depths of the human memory, Augustine makes the point that everything we know, everything we have ever experienced, every emotion we have ever felt, is impressed upon and stored in the memory. As so often, he makes the point that we cannot know something unless we already love it, and conversely, that we cannot love something unless we already know it. In the case of blessedness or enjoyment, which all human beings, without exception, seek, he observes that we cannot delight in and desire it unless we have experienced it and that we cannot experience it unless it also delights us and inspires our longing and desire to attain it.[20] What Augustine is attempting to illustrate here is the way in which God, who *is* our blessedness ('that is the real "blessed life" – rejoicing toward you, about you, because of you. It is the real joy, and there is no other'[21]), both transcends our minds and memories and yet must be present to them for us to remember, understand and will/ love Him. The question is: how? 'Where and when, therefore, did I gain my experience of the blessed life, thus giving me the capacity

---

[18]*trin.* 14 15.21.
[19]*Augustinus Lexicon* 1.166–180 (*affectus*).
[20]e.g. *conf.* 10.17.26–27.38.
[21]10.22.32.

to recall, love and long for it?' Augustine asks, for 'unless we were
definitely familiar with it', he observes, 'we would not long for it
with such a determined will'.[22] He concludes that before he learned
of Him, God was not in his memory, but that from the moment he
learned of Him, God 'deigned to dwell' in his memory (*et dignatus
es habitare in memoria mea*).[23] How then did he learn of Him? His
answer is couched in the language of hearing and listening: it is in
listening to God, the Truth, who is everywhere present for all to
apprehend, that we learn of God and God deigns to dwell in us, if
only we will rightly hear Him: 'Your ideal servants are those who
no longer look to hear from you the answer that they want, but
instead want what they hear from you.'[24]

What is it, then, that we hear when we listen to God? Augustine's
ecstatic exclamation – the famous hymn, or better, Psalm[25] – that
immediately follows these questionings, in chapter 27 of *Confessions*
10, is the answer: we listen to Beauty, the beauty which, when
we hear created things aright, we know to be the Beauty of their
Creator – the God who has deigned to dwell within us. It is the
Beauty that, because of our insensibility, has itself assaulted our
senses: shouting, flaming, breathing, touching, breaking through
our hearing, sight, smell, taste and touch, in order to inspire our
love, desire and longing.[26]

> Late have I loved you, Beauty so ancient and so new,
> late have I loved you!
> Lo, you were within,
> But I outside, seeking there for you,
> And upon the shapely things you have made I rushed headlong,
> I, misshapen.
> You were with me, but I was not with you.
> They held me back far from you,
> Those things which would have no being

---

[22] 10.21.31.
[23] 10.25.36–26.37.
[24] 10.26.37.
[25] As Hammond (2014) 135 n. 75 observes, 'What draws it into the category of "non-prose".... is not Classical meter or the medieval *cursus* but an antiphonal structure, which renders it akin to psalmody.'
[26] 10.27.38.

Were they not in you.
You called, shouted, broke through my deafness;
You flared, blazed, banished my blindness;
You lavished your fragrance, I gasped, and now I pant for you;
I tasted you, and I hunger and thirst;
You touched me, and I burned for your peace.

In this chapter I will argue that it is precisely this 'loving knowledge' or 'affective cognition' which the sensuous perception of music effects in our memory, understanding and will and which returns us to its source.[27]

Giselle de Nie's work, on what she calls (following Gaston Bachelard) 'dynamic affective patterns or images', the mental images which record or make 'visible' what we sense and feel, when we encounter figural or symbolic language, is, I think, suggestive in this context. The 'dynamic affective patterns' are images of, or responses to, what is often an intuitive, involuntary reaction which cannot easily be expressed in visual or verbal images, in words or reasoned argument, but which can nevertheless shape our judgements.[28] She further suggests that these images or patterns then reverberate in the mind with related images[29] (rather like the two actions of recognition and recollection which Augustine identifies in the operation of memory or the important role that we saw was played by authority, tradition and common consent in hearing poetry/music in the *De musica*). It is a process which can lead us, by association, to generate new images and discover hitherto unnoticed dimensions of what we experience. As she puts it, an 'affective understanding', a spiritual kind of 'emotional intelligence', has replaced 'reason' as the highest human faculty, and images (albeit neither visual nor verbal) are its 'words' or 'language'.[30]

But if, as we also observed at the beginning of this chapter, the images of affective cognition are neither visual nor verbal, what are they? What form does the image of something felt, tasted, touched or

---

[27]This passage is simply an example of the manner in which Augustine presents these ideas in many different works (e.g. *trin.* 13.6.25–26) in relation to memory, understanding and will.
[28]De Nie and Noble (2012) 1.
[29]Ibid. 3.
[30]Ibid. 5–7.

smelled take? What images do faith, hope and love take? What images do emotions such as joy, desire, fear or grief take? What images does the voice make?[31] When Augustine turns to the subject of the memory of emotions in *Confessions* 10, it is significant, I think, that he drops the language of image: in contrast to the images of physical objects, or the presence of things learned, he describes emotions rather uncertainly as ideas or perceptions (*notiones uel notationes*)[32] which remain in the memory even when the mind is not experiencing them.[33]

That 'affective cognition', based on sensuous perception, in turn affects our emotions and actions is clearly something Augustine was acutely aware of from his own experience, and he attempts to describe it in the *Confessions* so that others might share its effects. Thus, at the beginning of *Confessions* 11, he observes that he has related everything he has so far written, not to inform God – for he does not need to be informed of anything – but to stir up his own loving devotion, and that of his readers and hearers, towards Him (*affectum meum excito in te, et eorum qui haec legunt*), so that they may declare, as he has done, 'Great is the Lord, and exceedingly worthy of praise.'[34] Of course, the idea that the images created by sense perception were important in effecting an emotional response was a commonplace in classical literature, not least in rhetorical treatises where tropes are described precisely in terms of the response they are designed to achieve, either by making something present to the mind, provoking a particular recollection or chain of associations in the memory, inviting recognition, or inspiring emotions such as pity and indignation, love and delight, all of which would serve the speakers' goal to teach, to move and to persuade their hearers and to bring about a particular response or action.[35] What Augustine has to say about the emotional effect of listening to music in the *Confessions* should be read against this background. Like books 1–5 of *De musica*, it would have seemed entirely unexceptional to his readers. But what are we to make of it?

---

[31]Conybeare (2012a) notes that in *Gn. litt.* 12.16.33 Augustine refers to the 'image of the apprehended voice', the *perceptae uocis imago*.

[32]*conf.* 10.17.26 Boulding translates this: 'by registering themselves and making their mark in some indefinable way'.

[33]*conf.* 10.17.26.

[34]*conf.* 11.1.1 Cf *retr.* 2.6.1 *in eum excitant humanum intellectum et affectum.*

[35]Braund and Gill (1997); Harrison (2013) chapters 2, 3 and 7.

Music in Milan

Although written over a decade later than the *De musica, Confessions* book 9 describes precisely the period in which the earlier work emerged: late 386 and early 387 – the autumn Augustine spent at a country retreat in Northern Italy, immediately following his conversion in Milan, and the spring of his catechumenate, baptism and first encounter with the liturgical life of the Church.[36] Clearly, music was on Augustine's mind at this time. In this later work we are given a vivid and gripping sense of the dramatic upheavals which form the background for the quiet, even prose of the *De musica*. The two works hardly seem to be from the same pen, but oddly, and contrary to what we might expect and the way in which they are usually read (if the *De musica* is read at all), it is the early work which sets out the theological reflection which has been drawn from the very personal experiences which are described in the later work. We need to remember this early theology of music to understand how and why his post-baptismal encounter with the sensuous music of the Psalms and hymns of the Church had the effect he describes, for it is in the *De musica* that Augustine explains it for us.

Book 9 of the *Confessions* is, indeed, an extraordinarily sensuous book. Augustine describes his first experience of his new faith as one that assaulted his senses from every direction and which carried him on a tide of heightened emotion through some of the most poignant moments of his life: the deaths of his friend, Nebridius; his patron Verecundus; his son, Adeodatus; his mother Monnica, through illness, baptism, a miraculous healing, a mystical ascent. It was a time, as he puts it, of 'great happenings'.[37]

There are also a lot of odd-nesses in book 9, not least the very ambivalent way in which Augustine describes how and why he left his secular career as the municipal chair of rhetoric in Milan following his conversion. Sorabji[38] notes how closely Augustine follows the Stoic, Seneca's advice (*ep.* 68.1.3–4), on leaving his post in Milan following his conversion: he did so quietly, pleading ill heath, in

---

[36]Brennan (1988) 267 presents *De musica* 'as Augustine's extended intellectual justification for an intensely felt emotional response to music' in Milan.
[37]*conf.* 9.7.16.
[38]Sorabji (2000) 401.

order to lead a life of leisure and philosophy.[39] One wonders why he presents it in this way; was it because he wanted to set up a contrast between his very stoic, unemotional, retirement and his very Christian, affective, encounter with the Church in Milan?

Returning from the country retreat he had taken with family and friends, immediately after his conversion in Milan in 386, Augustine enrolled the following spring as a catechumen or hearer under the instruction of Bishop Ambrose. In undertaking the rigorous course of preparation for baptism which was standard practice in the early Church, he would have attended only the first part of the liturgy. When the sermon was finished he would have departed, leaving behind only those already initiated by baptism to receive the mysteries of the Eucharist. His experience of life and worship in Milan as a new initiate, receiving communion himself for the first time, following the multisensory overload of the long, elaborate and awe-inspiring service of the Easter Vigil, was clearly one which exposed him to the full force and power of Christian life as something to be *experienced* as well as understood: darkness and light, nakedness and white vestments; water and oil, bread and wine, incense, candlelight and shimmering mosaics. In *Confessions* 9 all this is encapsulated in three short words which sound like no more than an offhand comment, but they are in reality words which are so laden with meaning that they suffice for pages of attempted description: *Et baptizati sumus* – 'So we were baptised' (9.6.14).[40]

Given how much is left to eloquent silence, it is significant, I think, that what Augustine does describe in book 9, both in terms of its sensuous beauty and the effect it had on his soul, is the singing he encountered in Milan. Indeed, although he gives no description of the sacrament of baptism itself, he does describe music as a spiritual mystery (*sacramentum*) which cures his soul of pride.[41]

What he encountered was first of all the singing of the Psalms. It is no exaggeration to say that the Psalms were simply the air which early Christians breathed and the voice in which they spoke

---

[39]*conf.* 9.2.2–3.6.
[40]O'Donnell (1992) 3.107 comments that this probably took place in the large octagonal baptistery excavated under Piazza del Duomo in Milan and that 'by no later than Charlamagne's time, the legend had arisen that the hymn *te deum*' was first sung by Augustine and Ambrose, improvised as Augustine came up from the baptismal font'.
[41]*conf.* 9.4.8.

or sang.[42] They gave Augustine not just a Christian vocabulary
in which to simultaneously confess both his sins and his praise
of God's grace, but they also impressed a whole world of mental
images and affective cognition with which every aspect of his new
faith could resonate and through which it could be recollected and
expressed. Quotations or allusions to the Psalms appear in almost
every line of the *Confessions*.[43] The Psalms resonated in his ears,
were impressed upon his mind, moved him to lament of his sin and
to joyfully – ecstatically – confess his praise of God, together with
those who belonged to the Body of Christ.

This pattern of musical sound, resonating in the ears; perceived
by the soul; impressed upon the mind; apprehended by the memory,
understanding and will; leading to the expression of affective
devotion, is one that is fundamental to Augustine's theological
reflection; indeed, it is both the source of that reflection and what
it seeks to articulate and prompt others to share. In the *Confessions*
we are given a rare glimpse of the actual experiences of sensuous
music on which this theology is based. This is music whose beauty
inspires the love which *De musica* identified as the key to the right
use of sensuous, temporal music and the enjoyment of divine, eternal
music. As in *De musica*, the love which music inspires acts like a
weight, a gravitational force, drawing, pulling, inexorably moving
and inflaming the soul through the sensuous beauty of what is heard
or sung, towards its immutable source: 'My weight is my love (*pondus
meum amor meus*), and wherever I am carried, it is this weight that
carries me. Your Gift sets us afire and we are borne upward; we catch
his flame and up we go. In our hearts we climb those upward paths,
singing the songs of ascent (*cantamus canticum graduum*).'[44]

---

[42]Burns (1993) 142 notes the effect of the daily experience of reciting or singing the
Psalms in worship, where (at least in a monastic setting) the whole psalter would be
completed every week; Harrison (2011); Harrison (2015) for the omnipresence of
the Psalms in early Christian devotion and literature.

[43]Knauer (1955) offers a systematic analysis. In reference to the presence of the
Psalms in the *Confessions*, Conybeare (2012) 101 observes, 'The sound of language
in the *Confessions* is not just that of the spoken word: again and again it is the sound
of song.... Praise is sung, invocation cries aloud. The *Confessions* starts in a clamour
of ecstatic sound.... To describe the *Confessions* as song is not an act of whimsy:
singing is its natural mode.'

[44]*conf.* 13.9.10 Augustine is referring to Psalms 120–134 which were sung by those
journeying towards (the earthly and heavenly) Jerusalem.

This sort of music is first evident, when, immediately following his conversion in the garden at Milan, and before leaving for a retreat, Augustine tells us that he suffered a 'sharp longing for leisured freedom in which to sing with every fibre of my being (*ad cantandum de medullis omnibus*)'. What he sang was the Psalms, 'To you my heart tells its love: I have sought your face, O Lord, for your face will I seek' (Psa. 26:8).[45] Indeed, he didn't just sing them; he 'cried [them] out loudly', so 'inflamed by them with love' for God that he wanted to 'recite them to the whole world'.[46] In particular, he wanted to recite them for his former co-religionists, the Manichees.

Augustine was no doubt more than familiar with the Manichees' own extensive psalmody and hymnody.[47] His feelings concerning the Manichees are evidently still very raw: a mixture of bitter anger, indignation and pity that they are unable to hear the Psalms and experience them as he now does: as a sacrament, remedy or antidote for pride.[48] In fact, what he says in this context is striking: he wishes that the Manichees could have seen the expression on his face and overheard the effect on his voice, as he sang Psalm 4 during his retreat, so that, without his knowing it, and without their thinking he was doing so for their benefit, they could have witnessed what the singing of it did to him and the genuine effect it had on him.[49] For, far from being a performance for someone else's benefit, his

---

[45]*conf.* 9.3.6.

[46]Ibid. 9.4.8.

[47]*c. Faust.* 12.5–6. Many recently discovered texts have been edited and translated by Allberry (1938). See Burns (1993)140–141, who identifies traces of Manichaean hymns in Augustine's work; Puech (1968); Kato (1966) 239, for the influence of Manichaeism on Augustine's idea of an inner melody, heard by the ears of the heart, penetrated with joy by the voice of the Bridegroom (*conf.* 4.15.27).

[48]*conf.* 9.4.8.

[49]Kotzé (2001) Cf *ep* 9.3 Nebridius has asked Augustine how it is that supernatural powers produce in us thoughts and dreams. His reply is to say that if the emotions of the mind, aroused by such things as sensuous music and dance, can have such a powerful effect on the body, then how much more can supernatural powers effect the mind subconsciously, leading to thoughts and dreams? He writes, 'For, if it is evident that the exercise of our earthly and very sluggish bodies is able to attain certain incredible feats in playing musical instruments or walking a tightrope [rope dancing] and in countless other spectacles of this sort, it is by no means absurd that those beings that produce something with an airy or ethereal body in bodies that they naturally penetrate enjoy a much greater ease in moving whatever they want, while we perceive nothing and yet are modified in some way by them.'

singing was what he describes as 'the intimate expression of my
mind, as I conversed with myself and addressed myself in your
presence (*quomodo mecum et mihi coram te de familiari affectu
animi mei*)'.[50] Through singing Psalm 4 to himself, and before
God, he realized that he was able to find an outlet for what he
describes as the shuddering 'awe, ... hope and joy'[51] surging within
him, as he tremblingly took the words of the Psalm to heart and
realized that God's sweetness had taken the place of the bitter anger,
sorrow and pain caused by his sin. Reading 'the words outwardly
and experiencing their truth inwardly' he tells us that he 'shouted
for joy' and wished the Manichees could hear and see him and be
turned to the inward truth he now experienced.[52] He tells us that
each phrase of what he describes as the 'honey-sweet Scriptures
distilled from heaven's honey'[53] moved him deeply[54] and provoked
an affective response: the shuddering, trembling awe, hope and joy
which 'wrung a cry from the depths of my heart'.[55]

The language and imagery Augustine uses to describe the effect
of singing Psalm 4 is drawn from the senses of taste and smell: it
is sweet. Moreover, its effect is powerfully visceral, emotional and
physical: he wanted to sing with every fibre of his being, to sing
from the heart, to cry out, to give voice to 'sounds of devotion'
(*sonos pietatis*).[56] He is angry, sorrowful and pained at sin – joyful,
hopeful and set on fire by God's saving grace. His facial expression
and tone of voice reveal the inner transformation which his singing
of the Psalm is effecting in the intimate feeling of his mind. Within
himself, he senses the sweetness and joy of God's presence, which
has taken the place of his bitter struggles, as a divine sacrament
and remedy for sin. Thus, once again, we have sensuous music,
resonating in the ears; perceived by the soul; impressed upon the
mind; apprehended by memory, understanding and will; giving rise
to expressions of emotion. What is heard, perceived and impressed
as an emotion gives rise to an expression of emotion; in other words,
what is apprehended affectively gives rise to affective expression.

[50]*conf.* 9.4.8.
[51]Ibid. 9.4.9.
[52]Ibid. 9.4.10.
[53]Ibid. 9.4.11.
[54]Ibid. 9.4.10.
[55]Ibid. 9.4.11.
[56]Ibid. 9.4.8.

But not just this: what is comprehended affectively is the mystery of God's healing presence.[57]

'O let me, let me weep'[58]

We find the same pattern, when, following his baptism, he freely admits, in a surprisingly unguarded moment, that the beauty of the music he encountered in the Milanese church had a deeply moving and cathartic effect upon him:

> 'How copiously I wept at your hymns and canticles', he exclaims, 'how intensely was I moved by the lovely harmonies of your singing Church! Those voices flooded my ears, and the truth was distilled into my heart until it overflowed in loving devotion; my tears ran down and I was better for them'.
>
> (*quantum fleui in hymnis et canticis tuis suaue sonantis ecclesiae tuae uocibus commotus acriter! Uoces illae influebant auribus meis, et eliquabatur ueritas in cor meum et exaestuabat inde affectus pietatis, et currebant lacrimae, et bene mihi erat cum eis*)[59]

Were these 'lovely harmonies', these fluid songs, not what Augustine had in mind when he described that 'vibrant ... pure and liquid' chord we encountered in *De ordine* at the beginning of this chapter? Do they not evoke the sense of something beautiful and sweet which yet cannot be comprehended as reasonable or rational but simply as moving and affective?

We should stop here and reflect on the order in which Augustine describes the effect of the music he heard:[60] first, sound: lovely, sweet, beautiful song (*suaue* comprehends all of these); second,

---

[57]Sieben (1977) notes the therapeutic aspects of Augustine's emotions in response to God's actions in the Psalm and observes that it resembles Athanasius's *To Marcellinus on the Psalms* (which he argues Augustine knew). He also explores the evidence for Augustine's awareness of the Psalms in this period, drawing especially *De ordine* 2.22–23.

[58]Dido's Lament, Henry Purcell *Dido and Aeneas*.

[59]9.6.14 These tears are referred to again, as we shall see, in 9.7.16 and 10.33.50.

[60]Ibid. 9.6.14.

hearing: the singing voices overwhelmed his hearing – they 'flooded his ears' (*influebant auribus meis*); third, the soul's impression of a mental image: the truth was distilled (*eliquabatur*) into his heart ('distilled' here seems to have the same force as 'impression' – the essence of something being captured by the soul like a seal being impressed on wax); fourth, affective cognition of the image: it (the distilled truth) overflowed in loving devotion (*affectus pietatis*) – the tears ran down (*currebant*) and the tears were cathartic.

Like his earlier description of singing Psalm 4 at Cassiciacum the language and imagery in which he describes his experience of hearing the hymns and canticles of the Church are overwhelmingly sensuous. In this case, it evokes the flowing of water or fragrant oil – perhaps the water in the font at baptism or the oil of anointing used during the baptismal liturgy? In any case, it stands in sharp contrast to the way in which he had used the image of water and the sea in the second book of the *Confessions*, to describe the swirling waves of lust which, as he puts it, 'dragged me ... over the cliffs of my desires and engulfed me in a whirlpool of sins ... I was flung hither and thither, I poured myself out, frothed and floundered in the tumultuous sea of my fornications; and you were silent' (2.2.2).[61] In contrast, the sound of the Milanese chant is 'sweet'; it 'floods' his ears, is 'distilled' into his heart, 'overflows' in loving devotion, 'runs down' in tears. Whereas in book 2, Augustine observes that although God was not, in fact, silent, but was 'constantly singing' a song into his ears, 'none of it sank down into my heart ... to induce me to act on it',[62] in book 9, the voices he heard overwhelmed, informed and moved him to loving devotion and cathartic tears; the distilled truth, or mental impression, led not to 'intellectual cognition' but to what we have described as 'affective cognition', expressed in loving devotion and

---

[61]The image is one he sustains throughout book 2 where he refers to the 'stormy surge of my adolescence' (2.2.3), 'flood-tide of my nature' (2.2.4), 'dragged down to the depths' (2.3.5). It appears in the same context, in *ciu.* 9.3, in his reflections on Apuleius on demons, where he refers to the passions and emotions on which the demons' 'minds and hearts, like those of men, are continually tossing on all the surge and tide of passionate disquietude'. He comments that they are 'punished as they are being tossed..... On the high sea of their hearts, with no rock of truth or virtue to save them from the waves of their wild and depraved affections'.
[62]*conf.* 2.3.7.

tears – presumably the sort of tears which we have all experienced when something moves us so deeply that we involuntarily weep and are literally moved to tears.[63]

What are these tears? They are, first of all, the outpouring of an emotion which has welled up within the soul and involuntarily flows from it.[64] When we ask what the tears actually express, what the emotion is, then we are beginning, as it were, to cognize it. To reflect on how we do this is to reflect on how we cognize or apprehend music, for the tears are simply an expression of what the music Augustine heard communicated to him, how *he* cognized or apprehended it, what it meant to him, what effect it had.

It is significant, I think, that Augustine does not tell us what the music he heard in Milan was; he does not describe how it was performed; he doesn't analyse its rhythmic or harmonic/ melodic structure; he doesn't tell us which mode it was played in; he simply tells us that it overwhelmed him and that it moved him to tears. In other words, he simply tells us that what he heard was something he felt: he apprehended the singing affectively and it prompted affective expression. In the last chapter we examined Augustine's attempt to theorize this process, when we considered the psychology of musical perception which he sets out with such care and precision in the sixth book of *De musica*. What we found was an understanding of musical perception which we are now familiar with, in which sound reverberates in the ear, is perceived by the soul, inscribed upon the memory, and cognized by the natural sense of hearing as delightful or offensive. We suggested that the natural sense was later expounded theologically as the gravitational force or weight of love which, when rightly directed by God's grace, enables each stage of perception to be rightly directed towards love of neighbour and love of God. In *De musica*,

---

[63]Augustine uses similar terms later on in book 9 when describing his reaction to Monnica's death. As Natoli (2008) 8 observes, 'Upon closing Monnica's eyes, Augustine uses terms such as *confluebat, transfluebat, lacrimas, fontem, and fletus*' (9.12.29).

[64]*ciu.* 14.9 'We have to admit that the emotions we experience, even when they are right and as God would have them, belong to this life, not to the life we hope for in the future; and often we yield to them against our will. Thus we sometimes weep, even when we do not want to, though we may be moved not by any blameworthy desire but by praiseworthy charity. That implies that we have these emotions as a result of the weakness of our human condition.'

too, then, we argued that despite its rational form and arguments, the cognition of music was affective and, when rightly used and directed, found affective expression. In response to the question of what Augustine's tears are, then, we might legitimately answer, in the light of Augustine's subsequent theological reflection: they are an affective cognition of God's grace, heard in and through the sweet singing of the Church, which prompted in him an affective response.

Another way of tackling the question: 'what are these tears?' might be to examine how we cognize the tears ourselves, as readers of Augustine's account. Our cognition may well be equally affective; we, too, might be moved to tears on reading Augustine's account of his own tears. Why? It may well be the case that Augustine's tears prompt in us a recognition and recollection of just what it is like to hear music in this way, because we have also felt such emotion and perhaps even shed such tears, in response to hearing a particular piece of music. We may remember the occasion and the music, remember what we felt and thought, remember what we did. Our cognition of Augustine's account of his tears may also take the form of understanding: we may, reflecting on the account, contemplating it, mulling it over, be prompted to interpret it in relation to the many different social, cultural, theological, philosophical contexts which (like the 'authority of the ancients' we encountered in *De musica*) have formed the way we perceive things and which cannot be ignored. Finally, in contrast to the Manichees who may have overheard Augustine's impassioned singing of Psalm 4, we might cognize Augustine's tears on reading his account of hearing the music in Milan, by being moved by a desire to direct our own minds and hearts in the same direction as his; to imitate or, indeed, to share, his tears; to be moved as he was.

So, what are these tears? The short answer is: they are an affective cognition which prompts an affective response. Of course, the response is rarely simply affective: we often respond to what we have felt by acting upon it. Feeling leads to action. This is simply another way of stating what many ancient thinkers taught: that affective cognition, including the affective cognition prompted by music, can be the means of healing, purifying, harmonizing, unifying and transforming the hearer, their bodies, their minds and their lives.

It was often suggested that music was more powerful in prompting this process because it engages more than one sense.[65] As we saw in the early books of *De musica*, music was not simply something Augustine and his interlocutor encountered by hearing or performing it but something they *saw* when they watched a rhythmic dance or the movements of a hand or foot marking the upbeat and downbeat. In other words, music is expressed and encountered in sound *and* in action; indeed, one might argue that often the actions reinforce or interpret the sound, and the sound reinforces or interprets the actions. There is an eloquence, as it were, of sound and action, mutually informing and performing each other: the sound is seen and the seen is heard.[66] This is very much how Augustine understood the creating, providential action of God; it is at once action and sound, seen and heard – seen because heard and heard because seen – silent music, played out in creation and providence so that we might apprehend it, respond to it, and in responding, be carried away to its source.[67] This is also what Augustine's tears are: they are an affective response to the presence of God in the sweet singing of the Milanese church which carry him towards its source.

The problem with tears, of course, is that they are usually precipitated by an emotion which cannot be rationally comprehended, contained and explained; indeed, it is precisely *because* what is felt cannot be grasped, tamed and pinned down for inspection that the tears flow: they are the expression of a mind and heart flooded, overflowing, with an emotion it cannot contain. We are understandably wary of what defies or eludes rational comprehension or intellectual categorization, but we cannot deny (unless we are Stoics) that there are things like tears which do defy

---

[65]E.g. Aristides Quintilianus *On Music* 2.4 'How ... could music fail to captivate, since it makes its mimesis not through one sensory perception but through many.... only music teaches both by word and by the counterparts of actions.... These things are evident both from the dance of ancient choruses.... and from the things written down by many authors about delivery [he no doubt has in mind the gestures of rhetors].'

[66]What we saw Augustine practising in the *De musica* was a standard part of classical education, where students would learn how to scan and beat or tap out a verse (Habinek (2005) 79–82).

[67]Cf *conf.* 4.12.19 below.

and elude it. The question, as we have already seen at a number of important turns in Augustine's reflection on these matters, is not so much that we feel the emotion – in this case, that we weep – but why we feel it, how we feel it and how we act upon it. If we weep because we are overcome by beauty, feel it as the overwhelming grace of God, and respond in faith, hope and love, then the tears may still be involuntary and irrational but they are *good* tears.

Reflecting on this experience later on in book 9 (9.7.16), Augustine, I think, confirms this interpretation. He uses the same, sensuous language of sweet-smelling oil or incense when he tells us that before his baptism he had remained unmoved by the miraculous healings which had followed on Bishop Ambrose's vision, and the subsequent exhumation and transportation of the relics of Saints Gervasius and Protasius to the Ambrosian basilica (an act intended to counter the Empress Regent, Justina's, heretical (Arian/Homoian) enthusiasms and her attempts to take possession of the basilica for herself). Although God's presence was as tangible as the odour of incense filling the air he had failed to be moved by it or to pursue it; he was gasping for God but unable to breathe him in. Prompted, he realizes, by God's grace to recollect these events after his baptism, he can now appreciate why he had wept so abundantly on hearing the singing in Milan: for this was the moment when, following long resistance, he had finally been able to breathe in the fragrance of God's gracious presence and let it to take effect within his soul. His bodily senses, his memory, understanding and will, had been involuntarily overwhelmed by the sweetness of God's grace resonating in the singing of the Church's hymns, as by fragrant oil or incense, and he had responded with equally involuntarily tears:

> At that time [the discovery of the relics], though the fragrance of your ointments blew so freely, we did not run after you: and that was why I wept more abundantly later on when your hymns were sung: once I had gasped for you, but now at last I breathed your fragrance (*olim suspirans tibi et tandem respirans*), insofar as your wind can blow through our house of straw.[68]

---

[68] 9.7.16.

Augustine's contemporary, Basil of Caesarea, comments that the Psalms could draw tears even from someone with a heart of stone.[69] Indeed, it was a commonplace that the singing of the Psalms could soothe and calm the troubled soul or console and alleviate grief – a property which Augustine, along with many other early Christian commentators, often relates to David playing for Saul.[70] This is, of course, redolent of the way in which Plato and other Greek musical theorists describe the effect which different musical modes (*harmoniai* – the arrangement of pitches that make up a particular type of melody) can have upon the soul so that particular modes are related to different types of behaviour and character. As Aristotle observes,

> Pieces of music ... do actually contain in themselves intimations of character: ... for even in the nature of mere melodies (*harmonion*) there are differences, so that people when hearing them are affected differently and have not the same feelings in regard to each of them, but listen to some in a more mournful and restrained state, for instance the mode called Mixolydian, and to others in a softer state of mind, but in a midway state and with the greatest composure to another, as the Dorian mode alone of tunes seems to act, while the Phrygian makes men enthusiastic .... And the same holds good about the rhythms (*ruthmous*) also, for some have a more stable and others a more emotional character, and of the latter some are more vulgar in their emotional effects and others are more liberal. From these considerations therefore it is plain that music has the power of producing a certain effect on the moral character of the soul ... and we seem to have a certain affinity (*suggeneia*) with tunes and rhythms (*harmoniais kai tois ruthmois*); owing to which many wise men say either that the soul is a harmony or that it has harmony.[71]

Plato, whom Aristotle clearly has in mind when mentioning 'the wise who say that soul has harmony' (*echein armonian*),[72] in fact, deemed all modes other than the Dorian (which aroused bravery)

---

[69] *Homily on the Psalms* 1.2 (PG 29.213).
[70] Harrison (2011).
[71] *Politics* 8.5 (Loeb 264, 658–661).
[72] *Phaedo* 87c (Loeb 036, 298–299) where he describes the harmony of elements in the soul.

and the Phyrgian (which encourages restraint and moderation) inappropriate in the Republic which Socrates describes, as they aroused undesirable passions and behaviour and were therefore to be avoided.[73] Augustine is evidently aware of the much-cited story of the Greek oboist who, changing from the Phrygian mode to the Dorian mode, was immediately able to calm the exploits of a group of drunken youths.[74] Likewise, his comment in *Confessions* book 10, that 'all the various emotions of the human spirit, in their diverse ways, have their proper vocal and singing modes, which arouse them by appealing to some secret affinity'[75] *et omnes affectus spiritus nostri pro sui diuersitate habere proprios modos in uoce atque cantu, quorum nescio qua occulta familiaritate excitentur* (10.33.49), closely echoes Aristotle's observation that 'we seem to have a certain affinity with tunes and rhythms' and demonstrates his awareness of what had become a traditional understanding of music's powers.

Music therapy

Indeed, while Augustine's descriptions of the effect which music could have on the soul are clearly based on the theology of music which we saw him rehearsing in *De musica*, the revealing thing is that the foundations of this theology were so much of a commonplace, for both pagans and Christians, that they could almost be taken as read: it was a commonplace for both pagans and Christians that the soul impresses what is brought to it through the senses of the body as memorial images which, when cognized inwardly (intellectually or affectively), can affect the physical health or humours of the body, the affections of the soul and ethical behaviour; they would agree that what we listen to is therefore important for the health and well-being of both body and soul; that body and soul are a microcosm of cosmic harmony and can therefore be affected by it. It was also a commonplace

---

[73]*Republic* 397–401b (Barker (1984) 128–135 and appendix A on the *harmoniai* p. 163–169).
[74]*C. Jul.* 5.5.23 See Sorabji (2000) 91 n. 59 for the various versions of this story.
[75]*conf.* 10.33.49.

that, precisely for the reasons we have just identified, music was important in the moral formation of children, even before they were able to exercise reason. As Plato has Socrates observe in the *Republic*, in a manner which very much recalls Augustine's natural sense of hearing,

> isn't training in *mousike* of over-riding importance, because rhythm and *harmonia* penetrate most deeply into the recesses of the soul and take a powerful hold on it, bringing gracefulness and making a man graceful if he is correctly trained, but the opposite if he is not? Another reason is that the man who has been properly trained in these matters would perceive most sharply things that were defective, and badly crafted or badly grown, and his displeasure would be justified. He would praise and rejoice in fine things, and would receive them into his soul and be nourished by them, becoming fine and good: but he would rightly condemn ugly things, and hate them even when he was young, before he was able to lay hold on reason. And when reason grew, the person trained in this way would embrace it with enthusiasm, recognising it as a familiar friend.[76]

Furthermore, we might note that precisely those terms which are used to describe the existence, truth, goodness and beauty of divine Being and created existence – that is, form, measure, number, order, harmony, unity – are also the terms in which both classical and early Christian thinkers describe music. Where Augustine diverges from these commonplaces is, as we observed in the last chapter, in his understanding of the Christian doctrine of creation from nothing, his conviction of the fallen-ness of the soul, and his awareness of the need for God's grace. In other words, he differs from them in his teaching that it is God, the Creator, *Deus Creator Omnium*, who is responsible for cosmic harmony and equality and that the fallible soul cannot rightly perceive or be affected by it, and cannot rightly act on it, unless it is moved by

---

[76]Plato *Republic* 401d–402a (Barker (1984) 135–136). Aristotle observes that whereas other aspects of education are practically useful or necessary, music is taught for the simple reason that it is liberal (befitting a free man) and good (*kalen* – beautiful and noble) *Politics* 1338a9-37 (Barker (1984) 172); Plutarch *On Music* 26 (Barker (1984) 232).

the love of God, who graciously inspires and effects in it a right love and delight.[77]

The main exception to what I have described as 'commonplace' is, of course, the classical emphasis on the supremacy of rational understanding over what we have described as intuitive, affective cognition. Aristotle, as we have seen above, comes closer to what Augustine is describing in relation to the effect of emotion on the soul. He writes, 'There exist in rhythms and melodies likenesses, most closely approximating to the realities, of anger and mildness, of courage and moderation and their opposites, and of all other dispositions, as the facts make clear; for our souls are altered when we hear such things.'[78] And, of course, it was Aristotle who specifically identified the cathartic effect of certain types of modes, especially the more invigorating or inspirational ones, which are capable of relieving emotions such as pity, fear or ecstasy and putting the hearer's state of mind right 'as if they had been given medication and purgation (*katharsis*)'.[79] It is easy to get waylaid in examining philosophical reflection on the passions; it is probably enough to note here that, as we have just seen in examining Augustine's account of the effect of his own listening to Psalms and hymns in Milan, he himself accepts the passions as a necessary part of how we, as fallen human beings, relate – or better, are related to God – so long as they are rightly directed: so love, joy, hope, desire and longing for God; fear of sinning; sadness and grief for wrongdoing; compassion for one's neighbour, are all acceptable, indeed, necessary.[80] So, too, the beautiful music of the Church's singing, which distils the truth, inspires loving devotion, overcomes pride and causes him to shed tears of involuntary recognition of God's gifts and grace, is not to be rejected.

---

[77]Though the idea that poets, singers or players perform not through skill but because they are inspired or possessed by a Muse is also commonplace – e.g. Plato *Ion* 533b–535a (Barker (1984) 127). 'We should be in no doubt that these beautiful compositions are not human or the work of men, but divine and the work of gods, and that the poets are nothing but the god's interpreters, each possessed by whichever god it may be. It was to demonstrate this that the god deliberately sang the finest of melodies through the poorest of poets.'

[78]*Politics* 1339a11-1342b34 (Barker (1984) 180).

[79]Ibid.

[80]*ciu.* 14.6.

As we have seen in the previous chapter, the important distinction for Augustine is not so much between reason and emotion, and even less between soul and body (for Augustine maintains that it is the soul that affects the body, not the body the soul, in this context)[81] but between bad, sinful and wrongly directed emotion and good, virtuous, rightly directed emotion. It is, as he observes in *De ciuitate Dei*, a distinction between a good and bad will: 'The important factor here is the quality of a person's will. If it is perverse, these emotions will be perverse; but if it is right, they will be not only blameless but even praiseworthy.'[82] It is necessary to note that when Augustine uses the language of will here, he is not necessarily referring to rational judgement; in *De ciuitate Dei* book 14, as so often, Augustine expresses the movement of the will in the language of love, referring to charity, delight and love as prompting good or bad emotions, such as desire, joy, fear or grief, depending on whether they are felt on account of the self or on account of God and neighbour: 'a rightly directed will is love in a good sense and a perverted will is love in a bad sense'.[83] When it is not for the sake of the emotion itself, or for one's own sake, but for the sake of God or neighbour that an emotion is felt, then it is a good.[84] Augustine expresses this succinctly in *s*. 198, 'the affections of the soul are faith, hope and love'.[85] It is this distinction which we see very clearly in relation to what we have called the conversion of Augustine's affections in the *Confessions*: the emotions in books 1–4 are self-referential; the emotions in book 9 are for the sake of God or others.

Aristides Quintilianus, whom we encountered above, makes the obvious, but frequently overlooked point, that the passions are not easily controlled by reason; they tend to be more powerful than reason, evoking irrational and involuntary feelings and instincts, such as pleasure, pain or fear, which defy its control: 'It is not possible to gain very much healing from reason', he observes, 'when men are troubled by passions: for pleasure is the strongest bait, by which even the irrational of the animals are conquered

---

[81]*ciu.* 9.3.
[82]*ciu.* 14.6. Solignac (1983); Thonnard (1953).
[83]*ciu.* 14.7.
[84]*ciu.* 14.5–9 Cf *en.Ps.* 145.5; *Gn.adu.man.*1.31.
[85]*s*. 198.2 '*animae affectionibus, credendi, sperandi, amandi*', i.e. it is an 'ordered affection' – *conf*. 13.49 '*fidelium animam uiuam per affectus ordinatos continentiae uigore formasti*'.

... pain remains inexorable; ... divine suffusions ... fasten upon superstitious and irrational fears'. The remedy for these untameable passions, he suggests, is music: 'For each of these' as we have seen above, he suggests that, 'there was a mode according treatments through music, gradually leading unknowing persons into a correct condition'.[86] That the music can work unconsciously to heal unbalanced or seemingly incurable passions is precisely what we see being demonstrated in Augustine's account of the way in which his sinful, wayward affections were converted to love of God and neighbour in the *Confessions*.[87]

'Music for a while, shall all your cares beguile'[88]

To fully understand the role of music in the conversion of the affections from self to God and neighbour, we really need to pause and go back to the beginning of the *Confessions* in order to examine what Augustine has to say, in a number of well-known passages, about the role of the affections. I'm thinking in particular of a series of episodes in the early books, most of which involve weeping, and which prompt searching psychological reflection: his weeping at Virgil's account of the Death of Dido in book 1, his stealing of pears in book 2, his arrival in Carthage and reaction to the theatre at the beginning of book 3, his grief following the death of his friend in Thagaste in book 4. These episodes are full of very raw emotion; indeed, emotion is their subject: in all of them Augustine finds himself possessed by an emotion very much for the sake of enjoying (or at least benefitting from) the emotion itself: he was saddened if he was prevented from being saddened by reading tragic tales, such as the Death of Dido (1.13.21). He stole the pears 'simply.... to enjoy the theft for its own sake, and the sin ... we derived pleasure from

---

[86]Ibid.
[87]The way in which the soul returns to God and orders the rhythms of perception/ music in *De musica* is by the double commandment of love of God and neighbour; so, in *Confessions*, the affections are converted if they are guided by love of God and neighbour, rather than of the emotion itself or of oneself.
[88]John Dryden *Oedipus* Act 3 scene 1 (set to music by Henry Purcell).

the deed simply because it was forbidden' (2.4.9). At the beginning of book 3 we find him Carthage, not actually in love but in love with the idea of love, a love which found expression in sensual pleasures and possessive lust (3.1.1). Later he seeks out tragic plays for the same reason as he read the Aeneid – because he 'enjoys a good cry' (3.2.2). In book 4 he weeps following his friend's death because (although he is genuinely grief-stricken and has an abject sense of loss) he finds that being miserable and weeping in fact alleviates his own suffering (4.5.10). In all of these episodes, then, the emotion is almost an indulgence; it is something Augustine finds himself seeking out in and for its own sake – or more precisely, for *his* own sake: for the delight he gets from stealing, the enjoyment of lust, the pleasure of imaginatively entering into someone's sadness or the consolation that comes from feeling miserable.

These are all perverse, proud, selfish, self-centred affections which are based not on reality but on a self-created fiction, an illusory world in which Augustine is the most important player, 'trying to simulate a crippled sort of freedom, attempting a shady parody of omnipotence by getting away with something forbidden' (6.6.14).

What is the reality? How are these false, simulated, self-indulgent and vicious affections to be converted? The second part of book 4, following the analysis of his grief following the death of his friend, is a rather neglected, but very important, retrospective resolution to the acute moral dilemmas which his perverse passions raised, from the perspective of Augustine the Christian convert. In it, he reflects more generally on the transience of created things as a way of reflecting again on his friend's death. Here, created, temporal, mutable reality, including his fellow human beings, is identified as the beautiful work of God, the Creator. Although it gives pleasure, it must not be taken as an end in itself but should be loved as something that owes its existence and beauty to Him, and which only finds its end in Him: 'if kinship with other souls appeals to you, let them be loved in God, because they too are changeable and gain stability only when fixed in him' (4.12.18). An extraordinary Christological section, which really amounts to a hymn, sets out how the Creator God took human flesh to become part of created, temporal, mutable reality, Himself becoming the object of our affections – of grief, compassion, hope, joy, humility, love – in order to reform them and to lead fallen human beings back to Himself as God. The analogy which Augustine reiterates throughout this section of book 4 is that of sounding signs

(*signa sonantia*) (4.10.15), the temporal movement of speech, or a
line of poetry, where one word or syllable must follow the other
until the sentence or poem is finished, so that we are never allowed
to rest but must always anticipate and seek its end (4.10.15). As
he puts it, 'it will not be a whole utterance unless one word dies
away after making its syllables heard, and gives place to another'
(4.10.15). 'This is the law of their nature (*sic est modus eorum*)', he
observes, 'they arise and sink' (4.10.15). Temporality and mutability
are thus part of God's providence and we must use these beautiful,
temporal things, to praise God. Thus, he comments, 'Let my soul use
these things to praise you. O God, Creator of them all (*deus, creator
omnium*)' (4.10.15). Addressing his readers and hearers, he urges
that 'if sensuous beauty delights you, praise God for the beauty of
corporeal things, and channel the love you feel for them onto their
maker ... they are from Him but also in Him. You know where he is,
because you know when truth tastes sweet' (4.12.18). 'This is what
you must tell them, to move them to tears in this valley of weeping,
and by this means carry them off with you to God' (4.12.19).

It is no coincidence that the qualities which Augustine uses to
describe God's creation – indeed, the very line of the hymn he cites
(the *Deus Creator Omnium*) – are also the qualities with which
he describes music in book 9: beautiful, sweet, temporal, mutable,
rising and falling, revealing God the Creator, moving the soul,
carrying the hearer off to Him, inspiring *good* tears – and as we
shall see – converting the affections.

Singing in Church

In fact, the chants which Augustine freely admits affected him so
profoundly were indeed rather special. The singing of the Milanese
church was becoming famous: as we have already seen, Ambrose had
composed a new form of Christian hymn; he had also introduced a
new practice for congregational, antiphonal singing of the Psalms.[89]
Augustine mentions this new innovation in book 9 with evident

[89]Perl and Kriegsman (1955) 497 observe that 'a new style of choral singing arose
at approximately the same time' in Rome, Caesarea and Constantinople, as well as
Milan.

approval and an awareness of its far-reaching significance for the practice of the Western church. The effect of Ambrose's hymns, and this particular practice of singing the Psalms, on the congregation at Milan, clearly echoed his own experience: 'Not long since', he tells us, 'the faithful of the Church in Milan had begun to find mutual comfort and encouragement in the liturgy through the practice of singing hymns, in which everyone fervently joined with voice and heart' (*Non longe coeperat Mediolanensis ecclesia genus hoc consolationis et exhortationis celebrare magno studio fratrum concinentium uocibus et cordibus*).[90]

Reflecting on how the same congregation had sung during an all-night sit-in to prevent the Arians (or Homoians – in particular Justina, mother of the boy-emperor Valentinian) taking over their basilica,[91] he observes that 'it was then that the practice was established of singing hymns and psalms in the manner customary in regions of the East (*secundum morem orientalium partium*), to prevent the people from losing heart and fainting from weariness'.[92] He adds that this custom 'has persisted from that time until the

---

[90]*conf*. 9.7.15. Moorhead (2010) notes Ambrose's emphasis on the unifying aspect of communal singing; it is also present in Augustine. Cf *ciu*. 17.14. Williams (2013) notes similarities in form and function between such hymns and the acclamations which were used by crowds to indicate their agreement: they were formulaic, rhythmic, demotic, accessible to an uneducated crowd and had a unifying, socially cohesive effect. In this respect Ambrose's hymns might well be regarded as a threat.

[91]See Dunkle (2016) 45 and n.173 for a discussion and extensive bibliography on this conflict and its historical circumstances. McLynn (1994) 195; 201 identifies two sieges: the one Augustine mentions on the Wednesday of Holy Week and a longer, more protracted and largely self-invented one, at both of which the new practice of antiphonal singing was deployed. As McLynn comments of the former, 'we infer from another source [Augustine in *conf*. 9.7.15] that this was the occasion when he first divided the congregation into two antiphonal choirs: this brilliant improvisation, which was to be developed further during a later, more prolonged vigil, must have done much to restore the recently punctured morale of his congregation' (195). Murphy (1979) 143 argues that in his (now lost) *Contra Hilarum* (*retr*. 2.38) – a response to the tribune Hilary's objection to the liturgical innovation 'of singing the hymns from the Book of the Psalms at the altar either before the offertory or when what had been offered was being distributed to the people' – Augustine is 'describing the infancy of antiphonal psalmody in the mass as it was to develop in the Western Church in the Middle Ages'.

[92]*conf*. 9.7.15 The Arians had composed their own hymns – Arius's *Thalia* (quoted by Athanasius) is perhaps the most well known – which may have prompted bishops like Ambrose, conscious of the power of this medium, to counter with their own hymns. Certainly, Chrysostom was said to have done this in Constantinople – Sozomen *Ecclesiastical History* 3.16 (NPNF 2). Similarly, Ephrem composed hymns in response to those of his rivals, Bardaisan and Harmonius.

present, and in other parts of the world also many ... churches
imitate the practice: indeed nearly all of them'.[93] What was this
custom that had become so widespread? What does singing 'in the
manner of the East' signify?[94] The short answer is that we don't
really know; the more interesting response is to speculate: does
it mean the sort of congregational, antiphonal singing he has just
described (such as we also find in the Syriac hymns of Ephrem the
Syrian and Jacob of Serug, and which Basil of Caesarea mentions
and attributes to Eastern churches[95])? Does it mean using the
particular modes and manner of singing which were practised in
the East, such as we can establish from the traditional chants for
which we possess good, though somewhat later evidence, in centres
such as Athens and Antioch?[96] Or, on the contrary, does it mean
the sort of simple, recitative-type singing that was only one step
away from actually reading aloud? It is certainly the latter which
Augustine recommends in book 10 of the *Confessions*, at a point
when, reflecting again on the power of music to entirely overwhelm
the attention of the soul by its beauty, he loses his nerve and, erring
on the side of caution, instead recommends this recitative-style
chanting as having no less an authority than the great Alexandrian
bishop, Athanasius, as its exemplar: 'He used to make the reader of

---

[93]As Dunkle (2016) 46 notes, 'Augustine's testimony is corroborated by contemporary
witnesses. Ambrose's earliest biographer, Paulinus of Milan, also mentions the crisis
as the moment of innovation: On this occasion, antiphons, hymns, and vigils first
began to be practiced in the church at Milan. And the devotion to this custom
remains even to this very day, not only in the church, but through almost all the
provinces of the West' (*Life of Ambrose* 3.13). Other references confirm the ubiquity
of congregational singing: *en.Ps.* 149.7. '*Let them praise his name with choral
singing (in choro)* What is a choir? Many know what a choir is, and, since we are
speaking in a city, almost everyone here knows. A choir is a group of people singing
in harmony. If we sing in a choir, we must sing in tune with the others. If one voice
in a choir is off-key it jars on the ear and upsets the choir.'
[94]Fontaine (1992) 16–23. On the Western Church's adoption of Eastern hymn forms,
see Brennan (1988) 277; Sozomen *Ecclesiastical History* 3.16 (NPNF2. 2); Paulinus
Life of Ambrose 4 (FC 15); Gennadius *On Famous Men* 96.231 (NPNF2. 3).
[95]*ep.* 207.2. McLynn (1994) 201 n.144 comments, 'Like so many of Ambrose's
innovations, the practice was current in the east. Theodoret *HE* 2.24.8–9 attributes
its invention to Flavian and Diodorus at Antioch in the 350's; both its popularity and
the controversy it engendered are reported by Basil (*Ep.* 207)'. See Ashbrook Harvey
(2015) on singing in Ephrem and Jacob and Serug.
[96]As imaginatively reconstructed by Marcel Peres and Ensemble Organum, *Chants
de l'Église Milanaise* Harmonia Mundi (1992).

the psalm chant with so flexible a speech-rhythm that he was nearer to reciting than to singing.'[97]

I'd like to think that what Augustine means by 'singing in the manner of the East' is a combination of the first two: antiphonal, congregational singing, using the modes and manners established in the Eastern churches which had a more developed musical tradition and practice. What we can conclude with certainty here is that, however it was performed and whatever it sounded like, this particular practice of singing affected the soul in the manner which is now hopefully becoming familiar to us: as sound it was perceived by the soul, recorded in the mind, cognized by the memory, understanding and will and gave rise to affective devotion. In this case the hymns and Psalms sung in the manner of the East had the effect of encouraging an embattled congregation, ensuring they did not get bored during the all-night sit-in and giving them endurance and determination in a siege situation.[98]

It is clear from Church canons,[99] as well as attempts to defend the practice of hymn-singing,[100] that the introduction of newly composed hymns, such as those of Ambrose, did not go entirely unquestioned. When Augustine reflects in *ep.55* on the customs of different Churches in this respect, he draws attention to the fact that, at least in North Africa, it was the Donatists (schismatic Christians who represented almost half the North African Church) who had captured this new, powerful means of at once informing and inflaming, uniting and rousing a congregation, while the Catholics appear to have lagged behind with their funereal and indifferent chanting. He therefore offers an unreserved, resounding endorsement of hymn-singing, which, he observes, has no less precedent than the example of our Lord Himself:

> We ought by all means to adopt it, especially if it be something in defence of which Scripture can be alleged: as in the singing

---

[97]*conf.* 10.33.50.

[98]McLynn (1994) 201 observes 'Most of the hymns were designed to mark specific points in the daily round (dawn, early morning and evening, respectively, for the three Ambrosian hymns known to Augustine), providing a framework for the long days during which the *pia plebs* "stood guard". A round-the-clock liturgy was thus improvised, each day and night being punctuated by services and song.'

[99]Laodicea (363) 59; Braga (561) 12.

[100]Such as Nicetas of Remesiana's *De Utilitate Hymnorum*.

of hymns and psalms, for which we have on record both the
example and the precepts of the Lord and His apostles. In this
religious exercise, so useful for inducing a devotional frame of
mind and inflaming the strength of love to God, there is a great
diversity of usage, and in Africa the members of the Church
are rather too indifferent in regard to it; on which account the
Donatists reproach us with our grave chanting of the divine songs
of the prophets in our churches, while they inflame their passions
in their revels by the singing of psalms of human composition,
which rouse them like the stirring notes of the trumpet on the
battle-field. But when the brethren are assembled in the church,
why should not time be devoted to singing of sacred songs,
excepting of course while reading or preaching is going on ...
or prayer .... At other intervals not thus occupied, I do not see
what could be a more excellent, useful and holy exercise for a
Christian congregation.[101]

Although music isn't specifically mentioned, the stages which we
have identified in musical perception are again close to the surface
in the most well-known section of book 9 of the *Confessions*: the
ascent which Augustine and his mother, Monnica, shared at Ostia.
Through conversation they ascend from the sound of their own
voices to their souls, which perceive these sounds, thence to their
memory, understanding and will by which the sounds are cognized,
and then, stretching out towards God in longing desire, they attain
Him who is found both within and above them.

The praise at Ostia

Throughout this chapter, we have identified the effect which
sensuous music has on the listener as one which involves 'affective
cognition' rather than 'intellectual cognition'. The ascent at Ostia
is perhaps a good context in which to demonstrate this. The ascent
itself is often referred to as the 'vision at Ostia', and as we are all
aware, seeing is usually related to intellectual cognition: when we

---

[101]*ep.* 55.18.34.

want to say we have understood something we often say 'I see'. But as some of Augustine's commentators have noted, the ascent does not really culminate in a vision, in seeing God – literally or metaphorically – but is perhaps better described as an 'audition'.[102] What is it, then, that Augustine and Monnica ultimately hear?

The episode takes the form of a conversational journey, as it were. It is one inspired by ardent longing for God, for 'Being Itself'/*Idipsum* (*erigentes nos ardentiore affectu in idipsum*), in which he and Monnica traverse creation, the body's senses, their own minds, and then, transcending the mind, finally touch, with every beat of the heart (*toto ictu cordis*) the Wisdom they seek (9.10.24).

Augustine then retraces these stages, step by step, in terms of their 'voices'. More precisely, he asks: what if? What if these voices each, in turn, fell silent – the tumult of the flesh, the corporeal and spiritual images in the soul, every temporal sign which points to its Creator and which inspires their love for Him – and they were to hear God himself, unmediated, and 'in a flash of thought touch that eternal Wisdom who abides above all things' (*et rapida cogitatione attingimus aeternam sapientiam super omnia manentem*), then, he asks, would this not be 'Enter into the joy of your Lord'? (*intra in gaudium domini tui*) (9.10.25).

Augustine tells us that the object and inspiration of the shared conversation with his mother had been to discover 'what the life of the saints is like'. When the admittedly beautiful, inspiring but always temporal and mutable voices have fallen silent, I think that what Augustine intends us to understand by 'the joy of the Lord' is precisely this: the 'joy of the Lord' is the answer to the question of what the life of the saints will be. As he puts it in gloriously mystical language, the life of the saints will be one which is ravished, engulfed and hidden away in the eternal Wisdom which is its source, in an inward delight and knowledge, or delighted knowing, which is unending. He writes:

> If this could last, and all other visions, so far inferior, be taken away, and this sight alone ravish him who saw it, and engulf him and hide him away, kept for inward joys, so that this passing

---

moment of knowledge – this passing moment that left us aching
for more – should there be life eternal, would not 'Enter into the
joy of your Lord' (Matt. 25:21) be this, and this alone?[103]

As we will see in the next chapter, this rapt, ravished, delighted
knowing will not be a silent one: rather, like the other episodes
in which music or voices have led Augustine to God, it will be an
affective cognition which gives rise to the expression of affective
devotion: in this case, the expression of the eternal joy of the angels
and saints who ceaselessly praise God in song. To 'enter into the
joy of your Lord', as Augustine so often invites his congregation to
do in his long commentary on the whole Psalter (the *Enarrationes
in Psalmos*), is therefore an invitation for them to join their voices
with the unending love and praise which the angels and saints offer
to God in the courts of heaven; it is to finally and fully hear, and to
participate in, the eternal music which earthly music and voices can
only dimly echo, but which they inspire us to long for and to seek
out; it is what Augustine describes as attaining eternal Wisdom,
which is the source of all created things – the stillness of eternal,
unending praise. As Augustine puts it in *Letter 55*: 'The Alleluia is
sung, which signifies that our future exercise shall consist wholly
in praising God, as it is written: 'Blessed are they who dwell in
Thy house, O Lord: they will be eternally praising Thee (*Beati qui
habitant in domo tua, Domine; in saecula saeculorum laudabunt
te*)' (Ps. 84.5)'.[104]

So I would like to suggest that the ascent at Ostia is not so much
to a vision, or to an audition of God's eternal stillness and silence,
but to overflowing love and enraptured praise of God expressed in
ceaseless song! It could well be known as the 'praise at Ostia'. I will
substantiate these suggestions in the next chapter.

However, in contrast to the unending song of the angels, having
fleetingly touched eternal Wisdom, Augustine and Monnica fall
back to the sounds of their own very temporal voices, 'to the noise
of articulate speech, where a word has beginning and end' and to
inarticulate, unsatisfied sighing (9.10.24).

---

[103]9.10.25 Cf *enPs*. 38.5 where Augustine refers to 'the final reckoning, when the
Lord will say to his good steward "Enter into the joy of the Lord"'.
[104]*ep*. 55.28.

Monnica and music: Democritizing song

Philip Burton has noted that each of the episodes relating to music in book 9 of the *Confessions* also relates in some way to Augustine's mother, Monnica, and that in all of them, music is treated in a positive way.[105] This is, of course, not incidental. Monnica worshipped in Milan; she knew Ambrose; she would be familiar with the musical innovations Ambrose had introduced; she was one of the squatters during the vigil to ensure that Arian heretics didn't take possession of the Catholic's basilica and would have been emboldened and encouraged by singing his hymns; Augustine's account of her life occupies the central section of book 9; she shared the praise at Ostia with her newly converted son. As the powerful effect of Ambrose's hymns became well known there were those who accused him of bewitching his congregation. In a sense, this is precisely what he was doing: his songs were like a magical incantation which instilled the Trinity into the minds of those who sang them. He confirms this himself:

They also claim that the people are beguiled by the chants (*carmnibus*) of my hymns. I do not deny this. A great incantation (*carmen*) is the one than which no other is more powerful. And what incantation is more powerful than the confession of the Trinity, which is daily celebrated in the voice of all the people? They strive mightily to confess the faith; they know how to preach in verses the Father and the Son and the Holy Spirit. Thus all those who scarcely could have been students have become teachers.[106]

---

[106]*Sermo contra Auxentium* 34 in Dunkle (2016) 46. See Homes Dudden (1935) 293–297; O'Donnell (1992) 3.110 interprets 'thus all those who scarcely could have been students have become teachers' in a practical way: that 'when the (for practical purposes illiterate) crowd learns a psalm or hymn, they become themselves transmitters of the message to others'. I think that what Ambrose has in mind is rather that those who were unable to grasp the doctrine of the Trinity with their intellects were able to grasp it through their singing. Biffi (2003) 37 describes 'la forma poetica e musicale, che non solo insegna la verita e le imprime nella memoria, ma le fa percepire con la piacevolezza della musica e la liberazione del sentimento'. He emphasizes Ambrose's Christological devotion (56–60), referring to 'il senso della cristologia genialmente impressa e transformata in poesia e musica nell'inno "all" aurora' (58).

[105]Burton (2007) 143 (in reference to *conf.* 9.7.15; 9.12.29–31; 9.12.32).

That music has a unique power to give the mysteries of the faith entry to the heart is something Augustine describes in *Confessions* 10: 'These melodies', he writes, 'demand a place of some dignity in my heart, along with the ideas (*cum ipsis sententiis*) that are their life and in whose company they gain admittance, and I do not find it easy to determine what place is suitable for them'.[107]

It was this conviction which no doubt partly lies behind Augustine's own composition of a song, around 393–394, against the schismatic Donatists: the *Psalmus contra partem Donati*.[108] It was an abecedarian song[109] (each verse beginning with a different letter of the alphabet), with a refrain to be sung after each verse which set out the faith of the Church against those who were dividing and mutilating it. By presenting the faith in a simple, repetitive song he no doubt hoped to inscribe it on the minds of those who sang it, whether or not they were educated, literate or able to grasp it intellectually. As he comments in the *Retractationes*, 'Wishing also to bring the issue of the Donatists to the attention of the very simplest people and, in general of the ignorant and unlearned, and to do so in a way that would be as easy for them to remember as possible, I made up a psalm that went through the Latin alphabet that could be sung by them.'[110]

In this way devout, uneducated Christians such as Monnica were enabled to grasp the mysteries of the faith through hymns and songs. How? No doubt partly through the words, but I think most effectively, through singing them, through the effect of the sensuous sound of their singing on their bodily hearing, their soul's perception, and their memory, understanding and will, where affective cognition gave rise to loving devotion: to the concord of those who sing together in one voice and to the love and praise of God which music both inspires and effects in the one who hears and performs it.[111] As we noted above,

---

[107]10.33.49.

[108]Lambot (1935) 312–330.

[109]Each verse began with a letter of the alphabet – though Augustine only got to the letter 'W' (*retr.* 1.20). See Clark (2017) 432–438 for an analysis of this work.

[110]*retr.* 1.20.

[111]Sorabji (2000) 84–87, citing Poseidonius, makes much the same point in defending the way in which the emotion caused by music is not necessarily irrational: that wordless music, which involves no judgements, can cause emotions that do involve judgements. He writes, 'A hot water-bottle, which involves no rational judgements, can induce in me the rational judgement that the world is not such a bad place after all' (87). Alternatively, non-verbal music can evoke emotions which cannot be

the fact that music is especially important in the education of children is often commented on in classical literature, for much the same reasons. Aristides Quintilianus, for example, argues that children have a natural affinity for music before they can begin to exercise reason; that music is, as it were, a propaideia for philosophy,[112] since hearing music affects the will, word and actions of the hearer by means of the mental images it creates in the mind, the harmony and inflection it lends to the voice, and the rhythmical movement or ethical actions it prompts in the body, respectively. He writes,

> In actual trains of events deliberation comes first and speech follows, and after them comes the performance of the action: music imitates the characters and emotions of the soul through its conceptions (*ennoiai*) speech through *harmoniai* [melodies] and the moulding of the voice, action through rhythm and bodily movement. Hence education of this sort should attend most especially upon children, so that through the imitations and likenesses they encounter when they are young they may come, through familiarity and practice, to recognise and to desire the things which are accomplished in earnest in adult life.[113]

---

expressed in words but which are nevertheless good and useful. It is true that, even if we rationally know that something is the case (e.g. Aeneas knowing that he must leave his homeland) we can still suffer involuntary emotion: for example, Aeneas weeps with sadness because he doesn't want to depart, even though he knows that destiny will bring it to pass (MacCormack (1998) 116f on *Aeneid* 4.449, quoted in *ciu.* 9.4). So, also, in the case of Stoic wise man, which Augustine describes in *ciu.* 9.4. When threatened by a storm, the Stoic sage grows pale and shakes – in other words, suffers emotion (Sorabji (2000) 10 thinks that Augustine misinterprets Stoic pre-passions/first movements for genuine emotion) but is then able to judge that what he feared to lose is relative and that life and safety are not as important as justice (MacCormack (1998) 118). So, also, in the case of Abraham's horror and dread at God's presence at the sacrifice of Isaac (*ciu.* 16.24; MacCormack (1998) 118). The issue is not that we suffer the irrational or involuntary emotion but how we act: Aeneas departs; the wise man remains firm; Abraham obeys God. Cf *ciu.* 14. 9 'Sometimes, then, even though we are moved not by blameworthy desire but by praiseworthy charity, we still weep when we do not want to.'
[112]*On Music* 3.27 'We should assign to each [philosophy and music] its proper value and honour, and join them together in the most proper and legitimate union. Philosophy brings all knowledge to perfection, while music gives preliminary instruction:... music is an initiation, a gentle introduction to the ritual, which offers in advance a little taste of what is brought to complete perfection in philosophy. Music provides the foundations of every field of learning, philosophy the pinnacles.'
[113]*On Music* 2.4.

Music therefore functions in relation to children as faith does for the unlearned and ignorant: it is a means of acquiring cognition and prompting ethical action through the non-verbal, non-rational effect of sensuous sound on the intuition of mind, senses and body.

What music communicates, and what we learn from it, is thus more a matter of faith rather than reason; of affective rather than intellectual cognition; of the emotions rather than discursive knowledge. What we hear in music is something that moves us to attend to the music of every aspect of God's creation in a way that will not rest, or take anything as an end in itself, until we enjoy the Creator. In short, the affective cognition which music makes possible is, in a Christian context, another way of describing the operation of God's grace. The uneducated faithful did not need a rational, intellectual grasp of the faith; they did not need treatises such as the *De musica*; they simply needed to participate in singing it. This is, of course, as we saw at the end of the last chapter, precisely what Augustine himself concluded at the end of *De musica* and the reason, as we will see, that he ultimately decides in favour of using music in Church: because it inspires loving devotion (*affectum pietatis*) (*conf.* 10.33.50).

Monnica herself confirms Ambrose's comments about the power of music to communicate the doctrine of the Trinity to the uneducated, when she uses the final stanza of his hymn, *Deus Creator Omnium*,[114] in one of Augustine's very earliest works, composed on retreat before his baptism: *De beata uita, On the Happy Life*. It is a striking episode in many respects, but not least because what we are hearing is the very, very rare voice (perhaps even the singing!) of a woman – one of the vast, silent majority of uneducated faithful who actually made up the early Church; moreover, it is a contribution to what has so far been a very erudite, classical, school room-type dialogue between master and pupils on one of the perennial philosophical question: what is the happy life? Towards the end of the discussion Monnica intervenes to quote a line of the very hymn which, as we have seen, Augustine will subsequently use as the ground bass of *De musica*, and which he reverts to at important points in the *Confessions*, whenever he returns to the subject of music and its effect. The way in which Augustine presents his mother's intervention very much confirms

---

[114]If it was one of the hymns sung during the sit-in of the basilica to keep out the Arians, the Trinitarian reference would also be apposite.

what we have already discovered of the ability of Ambrose's hymns to inscribe themselves upon the memory, to convey the mysteries of the faith and to inflame the affections. He writes:

> Our mother, recalling here those words that still deeply adhered in her memory, awoke to her faith, as it were, and inflamed with joy (*laeta effundit*), uttered this verse of our priest: 'Help, O Trinity those that pray' (*fove precantes, Trinitas*). Then she added: Indeed, this is undoubtedly the happy life, that is, the perfect life which we must assume that we can attain soon by a well-founded faith, a joyful hope, and an ardent love.[115]

That Monnica most likely sang, rather than said, the hymn is strongly suggested by Augustine's observation that 'inflamed with joy [she] uttered this verse of our priest'. As we have already noted in relation to the ascent at Ostia and we will see more fully in the next chapter, spontaneous cries of joy, which overflow from the soul in song, are one of the distinctive features of Christian singing. Monnica thus brings the full force of the hymn, of music and of music's power to convey the mysteries of the faith without the need for intellectual discussion, to bear on a philosophical dialogue that seems to have so far left these mysteries unspoken and which has rather overlooked the role of faith, hope and love in attaining them.[116] It may well have been the first time Augustine had heard the hymn, but far from being disconcerted by this musical interjection by an uneducated woman, he appears to have positively welcomed, indeed admired, it; not just that, I think that he took it to heart and that ironically, it perhaps lay behind his beginning to write the *De musica*, very soon after, as an attempt to reason for himself just how and why her words/song (now confirmed by his experiences of music in Milan, as we have seen in *Confessions* 9) had this effect. Being a dyed-in-the-wool intellectual, he would never find it easy just to sing, to believe, hope and love; he needed to ask how and why singing worked in this way.

---

[115]*b. uita* 4.35.
[116]See Conybeare (2006) 89–92; Gerber (2012) chapters 1 and 2, on this passage, (he also identifies a reference to Ambrose's hymn *Splendor Paternae Gloriae* in Augustine's words on the sending of the Holy Spirit, which immediately precede this passage (p. 28 n. 39) (and which may therefore have acted as a prompt for Monnica)); Clark (2015) 99–106 on Monnica's part in *De beata uita*.

When Augustine returns to the *Deus Creator Omnium* in the *Confessions* it is, significantly, not a hymn he hears being sung, or one he sang himself, but one that his mind recollects and discovers within itself.[117] In the days following Monnica's death in Ostia, soon after the vision they had shared, the hymn which he had heard from her lips resonated in his mind as he tried to come to terms with his grief. The tears which he had hoped a bath would help release finally came as, waking from sleep, he heard the hymn sounding in his mind. This obviously recalls the earlier episode in which he wept on hearing the beautiful singing of the church in Milan: tears, involuntary, cathartic tears, which expressed an outpouring of emotion, an affective cognition of grace – in this case God's consoling presence and the hope of eternal life – were again the way he found himself responding to music. So, the death of Augustine's mother was not an occasion for tears of self-centred sorrow but rather for tears of hope and the reassurance of eternal life.

Sound and sense

What might we conclude?[118] Augustine provides us with his own conclusion in perhaps the most well-known passage on music in

---

[117]Moorhead (2010) reminds us that the hymn was no doubt known to Augustine and Monnica from being sung and heard rather than read. In this way, one might suppose, the already memorable structure and form of this simple hymn had been inscribed on their memories to be recollected. He also interestingly notes that for both of them, the recollection is likened by Augustine to wakening from sleep: 'One may place Augustine's recollection of these words when he had just woken up (*uigilari*) next to Monnica's recollection of a verse "as if she were waking up" (*quasi euigilans*) – perhaps a hint that recollection could occur when not fully conscious' (87). I think that the facts that the hymn was probably known by memory and that it can be recollected, as it were, unconsciously, are no doubt related. As Augustine's well-known reflections on memory in *Confessions* 10 demonstrate, he was acutely aware of the power of the unconscious mind – in this case reminding him of a hymn which describes rest as giving comfort to tired minds and dissolving anxious cares. The hymn's force derives, as it were, from the therapeutic power of memory.

[118]Like many ancient writers on music, Augustine believed that human beings are a microcosm of the cosmic harmony which music expresses; that perception of music through the bodily senses therefore resonates with the soul, affects the memory, understanding and will, inspires affective (as well as rational) cognition and prompts the expression of affective piety/devotion.

the *Confessions* (10.33.49–50). It is a revealing one, mainly because one senses a genuine honesty in admitting his uneasy ambivalence towards music. It occurs in the middle of an account of those sensuous temptations which still assail him, the new Christian convert, and which threaten his single-minded and single-hearted devotion to God (*continentia*). Taking 1John 2:16 ('the lust of the flesh, the lust of the eyes and the pride of life'), as we have seen him do in a similar context in *De musica*, Augustine works his way through the five bodily senses, and having examined touch, taste and smell, he arrives at hearing.[119] The fact that he immediately focuses on music and singing, rather than rhetoric, poetry or any other form of persuasive, emotive sound, is itself worth noting. However, having just examined the very dramatic effect which the music he encountered in Milan had on the new convert, it will probably not surprise us that it is precisely this landmark experience which he returns to.

He admits that he was even more enthralled by 'the pleasures of the ear (*uoluptates aurium*)'[120] in those early days in Milan than he is now. The high emotions seem to have subsided, and he confesses: 'Nowadays I do admittedly find some peaceful contentment in sounds to which your words impart life and meaning, provided the words are sung sensitively by a tuneful voice.'[121] More importantly, the pleasure does not hold him fast; he is no longer enthralled and the music is something he can take or leave.[122] And yet what Augustine goes on to confess reveals the more troubled and conflicted undercurrents of his experience of music even now, at the time of writing the *Confessions*, no doubt because he is still so sensitive to its powers. Peaceful contentment, sensitive singing and melodies which demand a 'place of some dignity' in his heart can indeed be a means of ushering in the ideas which their words express. But this is not always the case.

What Augustine is clearly struggling with here is how to balance the power of music to move the mind more deeply to devotion and

---

[119]*conf.* 10. 33.49–50.
[120]10.33.49.
[121]10.33.49 *nunc in sonis quos animant eloquia tua cum suaui et artificiosa uoce cantantur, fateor, aliquantulum adquiesco.*
[122]10.33.49 'but the pleasure is not so much as to hold me fast, for when I wish I can get up and go'.

to inflame more ardent piety, on the one hand, with the ideas which the words convey, on the other. How much does the emotion, which music spontaneously and involuntarily inspires, obscure the words or attention to the words? How much does musical sound obscure sense? We have already noted his comment that 'all the varied emotions of the human spirit respond in ways proper to themselves to a singing voice and a song, which arouse them by appealing to some secret affinity'. The question is how much this affinity can carry us away so that the mind is overcome and deceived by what he calls 'sensuous gratification' (*delectatio carnis meae*) – so that it loses all sight of the words and the ideas they convey, having 'grown languid' (*eneruandam*), or become sated, as it were, with enjoyment, and only realizes later that it has entirely forgotten the words or their message. The dilemma is a familiar one: what can we legitimately enjoy and what should we use? Is there a way of using and enjoying which does not take the object – however delightful – as an end in itself? The fact that music inspires devotion more deeply and inflames piety more ardently – that 'through the pleasures of the ear a weaker mind may rise up to loving devotion' (*ut per oblectamenta aurium infirmior animus in affectum pietatis adsurgat*) – is Augustine's reason for finally opting to endorse its use – for playing with fire, as it were – despite its obvious dangers.

Meanwhile, he admits that sometimes the dangers are too daunting and that there are occasions when, rather than confront them, he would prefer to banish 'all those sweet and tuneful strains (*melos omnes cantilenarum suauium*) which accompany David's psalter' from his ears. But then he relents; he tells us:

> I remember the tears I shed at the Church's song in the early days of my newly-recovered faith, and how even today I am moved not by singing as such but by the substance of what is sung (*non cantu, sed rebus quae cantantur*), when it is rendered in a clear voice and in the most appropriate melodies (*cum liquida uoce et convenientissima modulatione cantantur*), and then I recognize once more the value of this custom.[123]

---

[123]Moorhead (2010) 89 contrasts Ambrose and Augustine on song thus: 'Against the public and didactic purpose of Ambrose can be set the private and uneasy aesthetic response of Augustine.'

But Augustine the former rhetor and Augustine the singer of Psalms and hymns was more than aware that sound and sense, singing and substance, melody and meaning, delight and devotion, are inseparable: that one depends on the other and is enhanced by the other, that to try to separate them out or to divorce them was to lose both.

The episodes in which Augustine depicts his encounters with the music of the Church in Milan in *Confessions* 9 and 10 thus offer us a way of describing the effect of music which is best described as sacramental: the music is conveyed through physical sound, apprehended by the soul as a sensuous experience, described using multisensory perception – as a sweet taste or smell, as well as a mellifluous sound; it is apprehended affectively by the memory, understanding and will; conveys the mysteries of the faith; and prompts affective devotion. This is not to suggest that what we have called affective cognition is simply a matter of emotion but rather that the cognition arises *from* emotion: from love, joy and desire, or indeed, fear, grief and compassion – rather than reason. It is a 'felt' knowledge – a heartfelt knowing which prompts a responsive love – rather than discursive knowledge. As Pierre Hadot wrote, 'Dogmas are not mathematical rules, learned once and for all and then mechanically applied. Rather they must somehow [through exercises] become achievements of awareness, intuitions, emotions and moral experiences.'[124]

So, Ambrose's hymns worked their magic to instil an understanding of the Trinity into the minds of his illiterate congregation; Augustine's recollection of his hymn, the *Deus Creator Omnium*, instilled a profound sense of God's consoling presence and the hope of everlasting life. Ambrose's congregation no doubt responded in praise; Augustine responded with tears, but both were expressions of affective cognition and devotion: of the faith, hope and love which had been instilled by hearing the music.

At a number of points thus far we have found ourselves reflecting on the fact that, when Augustine considers the role of music, he is prompted to reflect on the operation of God's grace, a grace which is revealed in his works and actions and which inspires in us an inward love and delight – the 'love of God which is shed abroad in

---

[124]Hadot (1998) 51.

our hearts by the Holy Spirit' (Rom. 5:5). It is only through this grace that we able to delight in, to will and to do the good which has been revealed to us. In short, as Augustine concludes in *Confessions* 10, and as we will see in the next chapter, music, through the operation of God's grace, inspires our 'loving devotion'.[125]

---

[125]*conf.* 9.6.14 *affectus pietatis* Cf *conf.*10.34.50; *ep.* 140.27; *c. Jul.* 4.66; *en.Ps.* 124.1; 126.1; 145.4; *s.* 151.1; 156.7; *c. Max.*1.9.

3

The Conversion of the Voice

So Ajax and Odysseus made their way at once
Where the battle lines of breakers crash and drag,
Praying hard to the god who moves and shakes the earth
That they might bring the proud heart of Achilles
Round with speed and ease.
Reaching the Myrmidon shelters and their ships,
They found him there, delighting his heart now,
Plucking strong and clear on the fine lyre.

(Homer *Iliad* 9.217–224)
(Fagles (1997) 257)

'May the depths of our hearts magnify you,
may our harmonious voices sound you,
may our chaste affections love you,
may our sober minds adore you'

Te cordis ima concinant,
Te uox canora concrepet,
Te diligat castus amor,
Te mens adoret sobria

(Ambrose *Deus Creator Omnium*
Ramsay (1997) 170–171)

Augustine's contemporary, the grammarian Donatus, describes sound or voice (*uox*) thus: 'Sound (*uox*) is air that is struck which is perceptible to the ear, in and by itself. Every sound is either articulate or confused. Articulate sound can be captured in letters, confused sound cannot be written.'[1] It is a standard definition which Augustine probably knew from Varro, who similarly makes a distinction between a *vox articulata*: sound which is heard in letters or words, and a *vox confusa*: sound which cannot be written down because it is not verbal. In order to illustrate the *uox confusa* Varro gives the example of the whinnying of a horse (*hinnitus*) and the bellowing of a bull (*mugitus*). Shane Butler[2] notes that later writers added the roaring of wild beasts (*rugitus*), the hiss of snakes (*sibilus*) and the croak of frogs (*coax*), all of which, though non-verbal, convey meaning through onomatopoeia. He notes that laughter, clapping and finger-snapping are further examples of non-verbal sound which yet convey meaning. Butler's point is that Varro's *vox* is to be understood primarily as sound, not words – significant sound which conveys meaning both verbally and non-verbally.[3] He refers to the much-cited distinction made by Roland Barthes, in his essay *La Grain de la Voix*, between the singing of Dietrich Fisher Dieskau and Charles Panzèra – which for Barthes represents the difference between technical exactness and expressive sound, the mind and the body, words and 'the space where significations germinate from within the language and in its very musicality'.[4] Butler concludes: 'If we take the call of the voice to be that of matter, forever calling us away from the reduction of *voces* to disembodied words, then the world of ancient literature becomes a very noisy party.'[5]

Let's join the party!

---

[1] Cf Aelius Donatus (*c.* 350) *Ars Maior* 1.1 (Copeland and Sluiter (2009) 87) *uox est aer ictus, sensibilis auditu, quantum in ipso est. Omnis uox aut articulata est aut confusa. Articulata est quae litteris comprehendi potest; confusa quae scribi non potest.* Other grammarians such as Priscian in his *Institutiones Grammaticae* 1.1 open their works with similar definitions (Copeland and Sluiter (2009) 172–173).

[2] Butler (2015) 113–115.

[3] Butler (2015) 114.

[4] Barthes (1977) 182 cited by Butler (2015) 112. This is redolent of the distinction we have seen Augustine make in *De ordine* between those liberal arts which have to do with teaching and words (*in dicendo* – grammar, dialectic, rhetoric) and those which have to do with pleasure (*in delectando* – music …) (2.12.35).

[5] Butler (2015) 119.

Dismembering worms

In the years following his conversion in 386 Augustine wrote a series of early works exploring the nature of the soul. He was keen to demonstrate that, in contrast to materialist thinking, the soul is immortal, immaterial, unbounded by time or space; that its greatness consists in its force and power, not in material shape or form. This is the argument he rehearses in one of his earliest works, written just after the *De ordine*, entitled *De animae quantitate*. As we have seen him do so often in these early works, he draws on his training in the liberal arts, and especially in grammar and dialectic – in this case to analyse the relation between sound and meaning. Sound and meaning, he teaches, are related to words and their inward apprehension, to hearing and understanding, and to the body and soul respectively. Sound, words, hearing and the body are temporal and spatial; they can be mangled, dismembered and left for dead.[6] Meaning, understanding and the soul, on the other hand, are eternal and immaterial; they cannot be divided up but are everywhere present through their force and power. Sounds and words are therefore used to illustrate the nature of the body: they only exist in time and space, and if we take account of their constituent parts – their letters and syllables – they can be divided up so that they either no longer mean anything at all or mean something entirely different. For example, Augustine observes that when we divide up the word *sol* (sun) into its constituent letters, it becomes meaningless; when we divide the word *Lucifer* into its constituent syllables, on the other hand, it no longer means a 'star', rather the first syllable – *luci* – means light, and the second – *fer* – means carry. In the case of *sol*, the word is effectively killed off; in the case of *Lucifer*, however, the word continues to exist and to retain meaning in its separate parts; it is not completely obliterated but is merely left somewhat smaller and shorter.[7] All of this was familiar material for the ancient grammarian.

To illustrate his point Augustine offers the analogy of a worm, which, when cut into parts, continues to exist, though in a shorter

---

[6] *quant.* 32.65.
[7] Ibid. 32.67.

and smaller form.[8] The worm is like the body, he suggests, which, even when divided up in time and space, continues to be animated by the soul; it is also like a word such as *Lucifer*, which, even when divided up into its constituent letters or syllables, can continue to possess meaning. Corporeality, temporality and even fragmentation do not therefore necessarily imply the death of the soul or a loss of meaning. Augustine's point seems to be that just as the body, in order to be a body, must be animated by the soul and incarnate the soul, so words, in order to be words, must be animated by meaning and incarnate meaning. Likewise, just as the mutilated segments of the worm continue to exist even when cut apart from the whole, since the full force and power of the soul continues to animate them, so words, even when divided up into shorter words, continue to be animated by, and to convey, a meaning.[9]

How far can we go with this analogy? When does a dismembered worm stop being a worm? When does a dismembered body stop being a body? When does a word stop being a word? The answer Augustine wants us to give is: when it is no longer animated by the soul. Thus, for so long as the worm continues to move, for so long as body continues to possess life, for so long as a word conveys some meaning – however corporeal, temporal or divided it is – it is alive and possesses soul.

Our question then is, when does a word cease to convey meaning? Is it when its constituent letters and syllables are divided in such a way that they simply become individual letters or sounds, rather than words (like the divided letters of *s-o-l* in contrast to the divided words of *Luci – fer*)? Can individual letters or sound retain life, soul and meaning?

In this example, Augustine is keen to hold on to words but not to individual letters or to sound. But if the soul is as much present in the part as in the whole of the dismembered worm, when does meaning cease to be present in a word?[10] Is it when it becomes a sound which does not signify?

---

[8]Ibid. 31.62–64.
[9]Ibid. 32.68–69.
[10]Cf the later discussion in *s.* 341.9, where Augustine is discussing how the word of God could be both with God and with Mary, without being divided up. He notes that elements such as earth, water and air are in themselves a whole, but when divided up are present in parts which are not the same. Likewise, a whole piece of food, when divided and distributed, is given to its recipients in different parts. In contrast, when he speaks to his listening congregation, and sets before them food

I would like to remember these squirming bits of dissected, but still animate, worm as we move in this chapter to examine the role of non-verbal sound and of songs without words in expressing and conveying meaning.[11]

Humming along

Around the time that Augustine wrote the *De musica*, in other words, soon after he returned to his native Africa in 389, he was also preoccupied with a work which he entitled *De magistro* or *The Teacher.* It is a dialogue between himself and his teenage son, Adeodatus,[12] on how we learn anything. It begins with words: 'What do you suppose is our purpose when we use words?' Augustine asks (1.1). He suggests that 'when we use words we desire nothing but

---

consisting of voices and words, everything he says reaches everyone who listens, in its entirety. The whole word is received as a whole by everyone. So, significantly, is the voice: when someone speaks, the voice which carries words to us is present as a whole, to everyone who listens; there is no need to divide words up into syllables for all to hear it. This, Augustine suggests, gives us an (albeit) corporeal analogy to grasp how the Divine Word can be both simultaneously present with God and present in Mary's womb but without being divided into separate, different parts.

[11]Alexander (2001) 129–130 'Lyric was originally named for its parts. A *melos* was a limb and *melē poiein* at first meant "to dismember." The word *melos* was transferred to refer to the limbs or members of song – the repeating musical strains or stanzas which are the defining feature of lyric, and *melopoeia* now meant the making of lyric parts.' He cites Longinus on Sappho's verse: 'Do you not admire the way in which she brings everything together – mind and body, hearing and tongue, eyes and skin? She seems to have lost them all, and to be looking for them as though they were external to her. She is cold and hot, mad and sane, frightened and near death, all by turns. The result is that we see in her not a single emotion, but a complex of emotions' (Longinus', *On the Sublime*, 10.3, in Russell and Winterbottom (1972) 472). Alexander comments, 'Longinus helps us to see that the power of Sappho's poem comes from its ability to conjure up its speaker's somatic presence. The various body parts combine to imply a whole, but at the same time they are treated separately, each given its own agency and personality ... The Sapphic stanza, then, has always been a site where the parts – *melē* – and wholes of lyric form have represented the parts and wholes of human bodies, voices, identities' (130–131).

[12]Born to his concubine while Augustine was still a Manichee. He was sixteen when the dialogue took place and died shortly after. Augustine tells us that 'all the thoughts there attributed to my interlocutor were truly his' (*conf.* 9.6.14).

to let someone know something', but his son hesitates: 'Not quite', he responds.

Adeodatus's hesitation is evidently based on his experience of singing: we often sing, he observes, when we are alone, with no intention of telling anyone anything – at least, he does. Augustine takes his point and reconsiders, adding a second reason for why we use words: we use them, he suggests, not only to teach people something but to remind them of something. When we sing, then, we use words, not to remind someone else but to remind ourselves. Adeodatus, however, still isn't impressed: 'Well, hardly', he comments, 'for I very rarely sing to remind myself of anything, almost always simply to give myself pleasure' (1.1). Augustine again takes his point and is prompted to acknowledge that music is, indeed, different. What gives pleasure in song, he concedes, is the melody or rhythmic measure,[13] and although this may well take the form of words, as it does in Augustine's analysis of poetry in *De musica*, it may also be non-verbal: 'Flutes and harps make melody. Birds sing. Sometimes we hum a bit of music without words.'[14] So singing is not the same as speaking: it is distinguished from speaking because it doesn't necessarily communicate anything to anyone; it doesn't necessarily remind us of anything; it isn't necessarily verbal; it pleases because of rhythmic measure, which can be non-verbal. Words, then, communicate and remind; speaking teaches; singing – well what *does* singing do?

Augustine is keen to summarize and move the discussion on: 'You agree, then, that there is no other reason for the use of words than either to teach or to call something to mind?' (1.2). Adeodatus, however, is reluctant to concede. Thinking about singing has clearly prompted him to begin to think about another occasion when we use words or non-verbal utterance, when we are alone, not to inform someone of anything or to remind them of anything but to take delight. He is thinking of prayer: 'I would agree were I not impressed by the fact that we use words when we pray' (1.2), he responds. It becomes clear to father and son that although prayer

---

[13]*id quod te delectat in cantu, modulationem quamdam esse soni* – recalling Augustine's definition of music at the beginning of *De musica: musica est scientia bene modulandi.*

[14]*mag.* 1.1 *Nam et tibiis et cithara cantatur, et aves cantant, et nos interdum sine uerbis musicum aliquid sonamus.*

(like music) *can* be verbal, can communicate something to others and can remind those who utter it or overhear it of something, prayer (like music) doesn't actually *need* words; it doesn't need to communicate anything to anyone; it doesn't need to remind anyone of anything. God already knows and hears. 'He who speaks gives by articulate sounds (*per articulatum sonum*) an external sign of what he wants. But God is to be sought and prayed to in the secret place of the rational soul' (1.2). (Like music), prayer can be wordless; we can practise prayer in the 'chamber of the heart ', in the 'inmost mind' or 'inner man' which is God's dwelling place and temple (1.2). Here we can indeed use inner words or the thought of words, but Augustine observes that these words simply call to mind, through the memory, the realities of which the words are signs:

> It might be contended that, though we utter no sound, we nevertheless use words in thinking and therefore use speech within our minds. But such speech is nothing but a calling to remembrance of the realities of which the words are but the signs (*res ipsas quarum signa sunt uerba*), for the memory, which retains the words and turns them over and over, causes the realities to come to mind. (1.2)

In other words, prayer does not strictly need words; it simply needs to be a wordless intention towards God, an inward movement of the heart, which, through recognition and recollection – or holy attention – can directly encounter the realities which words merely signify.

The interlocutors in *De magistro* then move on to other things. The link between singing and prayer is not explicitly made (hence my parentheses above); the two are simply juxtaposed as two similar qualifiers of words; their nature, practice and end are described in the same terms, but the reader is left to draw their own conclusions. This particular reader cannot but reflect that Adeodatus, when he is alone, singing to himself, humming happily along without words, delighting in music, is like someone turning within to pray, bringing to mind the realities of which words are but signs, delighting in the reality itself; that whereas words are signs, non-verbal melody or prayer makes present the reality; and that singing and melody, like prayer, reach God without words because he already knows what we want to express and is both the inspiration and the reality which our singing expresses (more on this below). Singing, like prayer, then, is a lifting up of the heart towards God. This early understanding of singing did not leave Augustine.

Sign language

As we will see below, Augustine associates language with the Fall. He believed that following the Fall, the process of learning a language – especially a foreign language – or the skill of reading and writing is a sign of Adam's punishment: it is a matter of hard, penal labour. In the *Confessions* he reflects that, at school, these skills were instilled through the rote learning of rules, and when his attention wandered, through a harsh, coercive regimen of painful beatings. His natural instinct, he recalls, was to play games, to enjoy the fictional exploits and emotions of Aeneas and Dido in Virgil's *Aeneid*; instead he had to suffer the 'burdensome and boring' process of learning the elements of reading, writing and arithmetic(1.13.20) and 'savage, terrifying punishments' (1.14.23) to learn Greek words.

But we should note that in reflecting on his experience of learning to speak as a child, in the first book of the *Confessions*, he holds out a different model for learning which very much resembles the 'natural sense of hearing' which we discovered in the *De musica* – one that is natural, intuitive and able to judge whether what is heard is pleasing or offensive, without the need for rules or rational judgement, simply on the basis of listening to a voice reading, or singing, a line of poetry. He observes that, moving from infancy to boyhood, he learnt to speak Latin, his native tongue, not from 'teachers but speakers'; not through 'the painful pressure of people pestering me' but through 'the cuddles ... teasing and playful, happy laughter' of his nurses, in other words, through 'the free play of curiosity [rather than] fear-ridden coercion'.[15] He learnt to communicate, in other words, through observing, listening, remembering and imitating what people did when they spoke; what sounds they used to indicate something; what names they gave to objects when gesturing towards them, for, as he comments,

---

[15]*conf*. 1.14.23.

Their intention was clear, for they used bodily gestures, those natural words which are common to all races (*verbis naturalibus omnium gentium*), such as facial expressions or glances of the eyes or movements of other parts of the body, or a tone of voice that suggested some particular attitude (*sonitu uocis indicante affectionem animi*) to things they sought and wished to hold on to, or rejected and shunned altogether.[16]

The contrast Augustine is making therefore appears to be one between a natural and intuitive, playful, free and enjoyable way of learning to speak, which takes place through listening, memory and imitation and a coerced and counter-intuitive, laborious, slavish and painful way of learning words, which takes place through rote routines. He is more than aware, however, from his own experience even as a small child, that the latter are the inevitable consequence of our fallen-ness and the necessary, divinely ordained means for our reformation:

In accordance with your laws, O God, coercion checks the free play of curiosity. By your laws it constrains us, from the beatings meted out by our teachers to the ordeals of the martyrs, for in accord with those laws it prescribes for us bitter draughts of salutary discipline to recall us from the venomous pleasure which led us away from you.[17]

We are left to wonder, then, whether the natural, intuitive, unforced manner in which we learn our native language, through watching and listening to bodily gestures, tone of voice and facial expressions, is nearer to our un-fallen state than our fallen need for language. The fact that Augustine refers to the non-verbal gestures as 'natural words which are common to all races' suggests that he has in mind the means of communicating which human beings enjoyed before the division of tongues at Babel necessitated the hard labour of learning a (foreign) language. It would certainly place him on the side of those who argue that non-verbal sounds,

---

[16]*conf.* 1.8.13.
[17]*conf.* 1.14.23.

music and rhythmic gestures or dance, preceded language in the history of human communication – and to an extent still do.[18]

Things and signs

The question of how verbal as well as non-verbal signs signify is briefly examined in a highly theoretical way at the beginning of book 2 of *De doctrina Christiana*. What Augustine has to say is both revealing and suggestive.

Having examined 'things' (*res*) in book 1 he turns to examine 'signs' (*signa*) in books 2 and 3. 'Things', divine and created, are what 'signs' (which can also be things) signify. Drawing on his training in the liberal arts, and especially in grammar, dialectic and rhetoric, Augustine attempts to systematically set out, in a manner worthy of the schoolroom, the nature of signs. He begins:

> A sign is a thing which causes us to think of something beyond the impression the thing itself makes upon the senses. Thus if we see a track, we think of the animal that made the track; if we see smoke, we know that there is a fire which causes it; if we hear the voice of a living being, we attend to the emotion it expresses (*et uoce animantis audita affectionem animi eius aduertimus*); and when a trumpet sounds, a soldier should know whether it is necessary to advance or to retreat, or whether the battle demands some other response. (2.1.1)

All of these examples (with the possible exception of the last) are what he calls 'natural' signs (*naturalia*) as opposed to 'conventional' or 'given' signs (*data*) (2.1.2);[19] in other words, they work naturally and involuntarily and depend on observation and the memory of

---

[18]Blacking (1994); Potter and Sorrell (2012) 28–32; McGilchrist (2010) 102–105; Mithen (2005); Zahl (2015) 3 n. 9. Barnes (2013) 91–92 writes that, grieving for his wife, he discovered a taste for opera as 'a more primal means of communication' than the spoken word; that whereas operas had hitherto felt like 'deeply implausible and badly constructed plays', he realized that the plot's main function was 'to deliver the characters as swiftly as possible to the point where they can sing of their deepest emotions. Opera cuts to the chase – as death does'.

[19]*Bibliothèque Augustiniennes* 11.2 note complémentaire 8.2.

experience to be recognized: 'Those are natural which, without any desire or intention of signifying, make us aware of something beyond themselves, like smoke which signifies fire. It does this without any will to signify, for even when smoke appears alone, observation and memory of experience with things brings a recognition of an underlying fire.' Interestingly, Augustine also gives the involuntary expression of emotion as an example of a 'natural' sign: 'The face of one who is wrathful or sad signifies his emotion even when he does not wish to show that he is wrathful or sad, just as other emotions are signified by the expression even when we do not deliberately set out to show them.'[20]

But as in the dissection of words in *De animae quantitate*, or the conversation we have just examined with Adeodatus in *De magistro* concerning the nature of words, Augustine is keen to confine the discussion to one particular type of sign, which *does* communicate something to someone else, and that is words, the most common type of sign. In short, he wishes to confine his examination of signs simply to voluntary, intentional, rational signs, rather than being waylaid by involuntary, unintentional and largely irrational signs. The reader will remember that Adeodatus raised the question of singing simply for pleasure, rather than to communicate anything to anyone else, and that this was quickly dispatched by the conclusion that what occasions pleasure in singing is the rhythmic measure, which is often non-verbal, and hence that singing is not the same as words. Here, too, Augustine is quick to dismiss what he has categorized as natural and involuntary signs, including the expression of emotion, and in a very business-like, schoolroom manner comments: 'But it is not proposed here to discuss signs of this type. Since the class formed a division of my subject, I could not disregard it completely, and this notice of it will suffice.'

He then quickly moves on to the subject he wants to address: conventional or given signs (*signa data*), which for the most part consist of words. These are signs by which we communicate something to someone else, signs which 'living creatures show to one another for the purpose of conveying, in so far as they are able, the motion of their spirits or something which they have sensed or understood' (2.2.3). Of course, what he has in mind is words,

[20] *doct. Chr.* 2.1.2.

but before he gets there, he suggestively observes that 'animals also have signs by which they indicate their appetites'. So, a cock makes a certain sound to indicate to the hen that he has found food; the dove calls to his mate and is called to her in turn. Likewise, a man in pain cries out. Are these cries, coos and groans also conventional, given signs, voluntarily used to convey something to someone, or are they natural, involuntary signs which express the motion of the spirit without intention of signifying? Having raised the question Augustine does not pause to answer it: it 'does not pertain to our discussion, and we remove this division of the subject from this work as superfluous' (2.2.3), he comments.

Moving on, then, to conventional signs, he again categorizes them. There are three: some are visual, such as nods, hand movements (does he have in mind the beating of rhythm or chironomy?) or the gestures used by actors, which 'narrate things to … [the] eyes … like so many visible words' (2.3.4). Others are auditory; the majority consist of words, which have become, he observes, the most commonly adopted means of signifying something to someone else, but music is also classed among such auditory signs: 'The trumpet, the flute and the harp make sounds which are not only pleasing but also significant', he comments, 'although compared with the number of verbal signs the number of signs of this kind are few' (2.3.4). There are also other sensuous signs, in addition to the visual and the auditory, he volunteers, though they are even fewer. For example, Augustine intriguingly comments, 'Our Lord gave a sign with the odor of the ointment with which His feet were anointed; and the taste of the sacrament of His body and blood signified what He wished; and when the woman was healed by touching the hem of his garment, something was signified.' But again, he quickly moves on, not pausing to consider these extraordinary examples further but only to stress that, of course, most signs in fact take the form of words and that these verbal signs are superior to the other types of sign he has mentioned because, as he puts it, 'I could express the meaning of all signs of the type here touched upon in words, but in no way could I have expressed all my words in terms of signs (*Nam illa signa omnia, quorum genera breuiter attingi, potui uerbis enuntiare, uerba uero illis signis nullo modo possem*)' (2.3.4).

The consideration of words as signs, in Scripture and in preaching, which will occupy the rest of *De doctrina Christiana* (books 2–4), then takes over, leaving all visual, tactile, olfactory and gustatory signs; all smoke, tracks, and sounding trumpets; all voices quivering with emotion; all nods, hand signals and bodily gestures; all calls, coos and groans; and all music in flutes and harps, to one side.[21] But amidst these sounds, gestures and voices, we are left to wonder, (not, as Augustine does, whether the words can be expressed by such signs, but rather) whether words themselves can really express the meaning of all these signs. Can words really capture all that is expressed in the voice laden with emotion, the poignant dramatic gesture, the sweet odour of ointment, the mysterious taste of the sacrament, the gentle healing touch, the insistent cry of the cockerel, the longing coo of the dove, the agonized cry of pain or the delightful melody of musical instruments? Is the non-verbal cry or gesture; the smelling, tasting and touching; the sounding, moaning and playing, not an indication that in these instances words cannot express what is meant and that meaning only finds expression – voluntarily or involuntarily – by other means; that the experience of emotion, the odour of devotion, the taste of salvation, the healing touch, the longing voice, and the melodious sound cannot be confined or captured by words? Is this what makes Augustine so hesitant, so uneasy and so hasty to move on to more certain ground? It is unclear whether these sensuous sounds and gestures are conventional or natural, voluntary or involuntary, intentional or unintentional, rational or irrational. Do they communicate something to someone or do they just naturally happen to express something which it is difficult to specify in words and which it is therefore better to set to one side? Augustine isn't sure and doesn't want to stop to find out.

But the problem is that in mentioning these non-verbal signs he has, as it were, inadvertently let the cat out of the bag and it will not go back as readily as he would like. They linger in the nose, touch, taste, hearing and imagination, evoking a sense of what can be communicated without words from one person to another, at a level which is not necessarily verbal, voluntary or intentional, but

---

[21]Music therefore appears here only as something useful for the interpretation of Scripture: 'An ignorance of some things concerning music ... halts and impedes the reader ... we find both number and music given an honourable position in many places in the Sacred Scriptures (2.16.26) ... we should not avoid music because of the superstition of the profane if we can find anything in it useful for understanding Scripture' (2.17.28).

non-verbal, involuntary and unintentional – emotional, poignant, passionate and purifying – and just as forceful and just as powerful for that.

Why, we must therefore ask, is Augustine so determined to leave such signs behind, to minimize their importance, and to concentrate simply on words? He has admitted that there are, indeed, more ways to communicate than words, but he wants to insist that they are few and far between and cannot capture what words express. Of course, all of this is, to a large extent, true, but is it reason for dismissing such signs and setting them to one side? His subject in the *De doctrina Christiana* is Scripture: the interpretation of Scripture and the communication of it through exegesis and preaching, and so his focus is indeed, necessarily, on words. No doubt our frustration that Augustine does not linger long enough over the question of non-verbal sound is our problem, not his – at least in this context.

Anyone who reads the *De doctrina Christiana* closely, however, will soon realize that Augustine's concentration on words – and especially the words of Scripture – continually leads him, not to 'things', or to a meaning which can be readily articulated, but to love: love of God and love of neighbour, love of the Creator who is ineffable and unknowable, love of our neighbour in and towards God. Indeed, he repeatedly makes the point that the only true meaning of Scripture is the double commandment of love of God and love of neighbour.[22] This, he insists, *is* the literal meaning of Scripture; if a passage teaches anything else then it must be interpreted figuratively.[23] Words therefore serve, not to communicate some 'thing' or some meaning to someone else but to unite the speaker and the hearer in love of God and neighbour. Words, in other words, become 'non-words': non-verbal expressions of love, communicators of love. They become expressions of shared desire, longing, delight and pleasure in the God who is love – a way of relating to and participating in Him through teaching and listening.[24] In short, what words express is indeed the meaning expressed by the non-verbal signs Augustine has set to one side:

[22]*doc. Chr.* 1.36.40.
[23]*doc. Chr.* 3.10.14.
[24]*doc. Chr.* prologue 6.

an involuntary, unintentional, otherwise inarticulable expression of love – or what we have elsewhere found him referring to as 'loving devotion'.[25]

Besides, words do not *always* take centre stage. In this chapter I would like to turn to consider more closely those occasions when Augustine does, indeed, stop and allow himself and his hearers and readers time to dwell on non-verbal sound, on music and – most especially – on singing, precisely for the reason that he dissected the worm in *De animae quantitate* or turned to consider prayer in the *De magistro*; or insists that the meaning of Scripture is love of God and love of neighbour in *De doctrina Christiana*; or remembers the playful, happy laughter of his nurses in the *Confessions*: because these parts, sounds, verbal and non-verbal voices convey the full, indivisible force and power of the soul; the delightful presence of God uniting those who hear with their neighbour and with Himself. They are the voice of the heart.

Singing the songs of David

Then let me retire to my private room and sing my songs of love to you, giving vent to my inarticulate groans as I walk my pilgrim way, remembering Jerusalem and lifting up my heart toward her. To her would I stretch out, to Jerusalem my homeland, Jerusalem my mother, and to you who are her ruler, her illuminator, Father, guardian and husband, her chaste intense delight, her unshakeable joy: to you who are the fullness of good things beyond all telling, and all good things at once, because you are the One supreme and true God. (*conf.* 12.16.23)

---

[25]Conybeare (2012a) attends to the sound of the speaking voice which, she argues (following De Nie (see last chapter)), often brings about an affective, non-rational response. She links this with the immateriality of God, who cannot be seen with our eyes but must rather, as she puts it, be 'seen with the ears' (146). Materiality – in gesture, sound, the voice of praise, and most especially, in temporal, faltering words – is, she argues, essential for Augustine in attempting to demonstrate the eternal transcendence of God.

There was one context in which Augustine seems to have been much less reluctant to let go of words and to allow the voice to sing out in sound that was not always verbal, and that was the Psalms. They were, after all, songs; the songs of David, and as we have already observed, they had become written into, and were sung out of, early Christian devotion and worship. The Psalms had effectively become the hymn book of the church, sung at every hour and office.[26] Inspiring and filling the minds of early Christians with their poetry, imagery and very human feelings, they were breathed out in song which punctuated every act of daily life, from rising in the morning, sitting down to eat, to going to bed at night (or keeping an all-night vigil). They were sung by every type of person: the educated and uneducated, young and old, male and female, in all their different occupations; they expressed every human emotion, every need, every movement of the soul, every feeling of devotion. In short, they gave voice to the meditations and movements of the heart.[27]

For Augustine, as for so many of his contemporaries, the Psalms proved to be songs which, as it were, overcame the temporal, mutable, material constraints of human language and enabled the believer to reach out towards the eternal, immutable, transcendent God in prayer and praise. In this chapter I will argue that song – both verbal and non-verbal – was the key to this. As we will see, in contrast to Augustine's determined refusal to concentrate on anything but words, his fear of being overcome by melody at the expense of words, and his ambivalent to-ing and fro-ing about singing in Church, the Psalms seem to have prompted him to drop his defences and brought out his wild side. In his readiness to embrace spontaneous, involuntary, undeliberated, non-verbal sound, – to simply sing in cries of wordless joy – we discover another Augustine: one who is prepared to relinquish words in order to embrace what words cannot fully comprehend.

---

[26]*conf.* 9.12.31. There are also numerous examples of extra-liturgical use of the Psalms in Augustine, e.g. in *conf.* 9.12.31, Evodius takes up a psalter and the household join him in singing Psalm 100:1 following Monnica's death: *en.Ps* 66.6; 137.10; *op. mon* 17.20 where Augustine advises his monks (and others *s.* 256.1–3) to sing when they are travelling – whether riding or walking – just as they do when working at home.
[27]These qualities are enumerated in Pseudo-Chrysostom *De poenitentia* (cited by McKinnon (1987–90) and discussed by Athanasius in his *Letter to Marcellinus*. Harrison (2011); Kolbet (2006) for further consideration.

Why did the Psalms have this effect? I think the main reason is that the Psalms, as Scripture, and perhaps most importantly, as prayers, provided a context in which words could safely be allowed to reach their limits, to 'slip, slide and break with imprecision', and then, to be broken open, become non-words, bringing the one who utters them into the presence of Him who already knows what they falteringly attempt to express and does not need to be informed of what they strain to communicate. In other words, the Psalms are like the bits of dissected worm in which the soul is still fully present; like the prayer, described in *De magistro*, which simply allows us to be in the presence of God, without the need for words; like the non-verbal, unintentional, involuntary cacophony of sensuous signs, sounds and voices which were set to one side in *De doctrina Christiana*. But in this case, reciting, singing, performing the Psalms, Augustine does not reject them or set them to one side. Rather, he embraces them as those signs, sounds and voices which alone can express what words cannot express: the voice of the heart, the new song, the song of the lover for the beloved, of the pilgrim on the path to the heavenly Jerusalem, or of the believer in praise of the unknowable and ineffable God. It is as if the Psalms provided Augustine with an entire world of signs, images, emotions, sounds and voices in which affective cognition of the unknowable and ineffable God could find expression in loving devotion.

What was this affective cognition and devotion? I think we might usefully revisit the categories we used to analyse the nature of music in the first chapter while examining the *De musica* and reconsider them here in relation to song – in other words, in relation to the music which early Christians actually used in a devotional context.

An ontology of music: A resounding belch

Rather than using the ontological categories of cosmic harmony – measure, number and weight; wisdom, goodness and beauty; form or rhythm – the one, fundamental ontological reality by which fallen human beings are able to apprehend and relate to their Creator is, as we discovered in book 6 of *De musica*, love. This is no less true of the later, wilder Augustine, whose understanding of the nature and consequences of the Fall, and of human kind's need for grace, did not change. We know God, he insists, not through reasoned judgement but through a natural, intuitive sense which is no more and no less than the love of God which brings creation into being and orders and sustains it; the love of God which is shed abroad in our hearts by the Holy Spirit and which inspires our love and delight in Himself; the love of God, incarnate, who redeems us through loving us with a self-sacrificing love which inspires our own love in return; the love by which God loves Himself through us and we love our neighbour in and towards Him; the love that will rest in nothing and take nothing as an end, until it returns to its source. It is, in short, the weight of creating, sustaining, redeeming love, carrying us – as spontaneously, inexorably and involuntarily as oil floats to the top of water, or apples fall to the ground – towards its source and end.

We know these aspects of Augustine's theology well, but music is rarely considered in this context. The two are brought together in a sermon on the opening words of Psalm 44: *eructavit cor meum uerbum bonum*, 'My heart overflows with a good word.' Augustine offers us two interpretations: the first describes the eternal begetting (*generationem Filii*) of the Word of God from the heart or innermost being (*ex intimo suo)* of the Father[28]; the second describes the eruption of a hymn of praise which arises from the heart of the believer in praise of the Creator and in thanksgiving and delight for His beauty: '"My heart overflows with a good word," would be the prophet's way of announcing his hymn (*dicente hymnum*) (for when anyone sings a hymn to God, his or her heart is blurting out a good word) ... the duty of every human being is to praise God.'[29] In both the case of the eternally begotten Word of the Father and the words of human praise which spring up in the heart of the believer, a word is begotten – a word spontaneously overflows from the heart, for this is the eternal nature of God and the nature of His love: 'Let your work be praise offered to God; let your heart overflow with this good word. Tell your works to the King, because the King has created you for this purpose, and himself given you

---

[28]*en.Ps.* 44.5 'From where does God bring forth a Word, if not from his heart, from his innermost being?'
[29]Ibid. 44.9.

what you are to offer him. Give back to him his own gifts (*et ipse donauit quod offerres*).'[30]

The spontaneous and involuntary quality of this overflowing is captured by 'eructauit', and it is perhaps this somewhat unusual word that prompted Augustine's rather unusual interpretation. *Eructare* literally means 'to belch' – and there are few things more spontaneous and involuntary than a belch: it simply bursts forth, unbidden, in a wordless sound. Augustine's point is that this is precisely what enables it to express the otherwise ineffable mysteries of the Godhead: the eternal Word is not begotten and brought forth in ordered prose but is belched forth from God's innermost being; our praise does not take the form of ordered words but bursts forth from our heart in wordless sound. Commenting on the natures of Christ in sermon 341, Augustine makes a similar point when reflecting on Christ's eternal Godhead, which is set out so wondrously, he comments, in the prologue of John's Gospel: 'In the beginning was the Word and the Word was with God and the Word was God.' He suggests that these words – which attempt to express the unknowable and ineffable mystery of the Godhead – are, in reality, a belch, a spontaneous, involuntary utterance of what transcends words. Resting his head on our Lord's breast at the Last Supper he suggests that John, the beloved disciple, drank in the mysteries of Christ's Godhead and 'having drunk his fill, gave a good belch, and that very belch is the gospel'.[31] All preaching shares the same quality, he observes: it is a belching out of what the preacher has been given to drink and eat by God's abundant grace:

> So eat, that you may belch; so receive, that you may give. When you learn, you are eating it; when you teach, you are belching it forth; when you listen, you are eating; and when you preach, you are belching it forth ... What have you done for us, Lord? You have granted us existence and enabled us to praise you and to exult in your holiness and to belch forth the memory of the abundance of your sweetness. All this you have done for us, Lord, you whom we praise. Let us tell of it and praise you in the telling.[32]

---

[30]Ibid. 44.9.
[31]*s.* 341.5 (Dolbeau 22).
[32]*en.Ps.* 144.9–10.

A belch – a rude and crude sound, an uncontainable, expressive noise of overflowing fullness – is, then, Augustine's attempt to express something of the ontology of love and the nature of song.[33]

A psychology of music: Singing for joy

It should not surprise us to find that Augustine, as a former rhetor, and then a Christian bishop, teacher and preacher, often uses reflection on how we understand and communicate meaning, and especially a consideration of the nature of language, in order to illustrate theological ideas. Language, he often observes, is a vehicle, which conveys what is in our own mind to the mind of another; words are the form in which inward understanding is conveyed so that others can apprehend it. How successful language is in this task is a question which clearly haunts him, however, and the uncertainty underlies almost everything he writes and says. He is acutely aware of just how limited language is: it is an arbitrary, human invention, which depends on authority, human agreement and practice, to mean anything at all. It is temporal and mutable, open to misinterpretation, capable of dissembling. Moreover, it is fractured and fragmented so that different peoples speak different languages. There is a fundamental mismatch, then, between what we know and understand firmly and clearly within and the crude, rude vehicle of human speech by which it must be conveyed to another.[34] Any utterance, he observes, risks a 'shipwreck of misrepresentation'.[35] Words can indeed teach, delight and persuade; they can also lie, seduce and mislead. Yet they are all we fallen human beings have.[36]

---

[33]We should perhaps remember that in some cultures a belch is a necessary and expected mark of satisfaction and thanks: it indicates that someone is happily replete. This would, of course, make more sense of Augustine's comments.

[34]Harrison (1992) 59–63; Markus (1995); Rist (1994).

[35]c.Acad. 1.5.

[36]And of course, Augustine exploits these limitations, as he exploits the non-verbal nature of music. His exegesis of Scripture, as we have seen, is effectively an effacing or breaking open of words in order to discover, as far as possible, their ineffable inspiration and meaning. Obscurity, ambiguity, figurative, spiritual exegesis are all

But we have already glimpsed – or more precisely, caught the feint echo of – an alternative: might the sound of the voice – and most especially the sound of the voice in song – not take up where words fail and fall, the *uox confusa* take up where the *uox articulata* falters? In his reflections on the Psalms, the songs of David, Augustine is prompted to explore this alternative at some length. First of all, as we have seen, there is a sense in which, even after the Fall, the believer calls, cries out and addresses God. They do so not with words, but, like Susannah, 'who', Augustine observes, 'was silent but cried to heaven in her heart',[37] inwardly, silently and in the depths of the heart – in other words, in prayer: 'If we have prepared within ourselves a guest chamber or house for God', he writes, 'we talk with him there, and there our prayer is heard', for 'he is not far from any one of us, he in whom we live and move have our being' (Acts 17.27–28).[38] Praying in God's presence, Augustine observes that we address Him with an inner mouth,[39] singing, calling and crying to Him, expressing our love and joy and petitions, not with words but with the intention and affection of the heart:

> *With my voice I have cried to the Lord.* That is, not with the voice of my body, which is produced with the noise of reverberating air, but with the voice of the heart, which is unheard by other people but makes a noise which to God is like shouting ....The

---

examples of this: they are providential stumbling blocks; the means by which the reader is humbled and moved to search out, delight and participate in the mystery of the God whom they simultaneously veil and reveal; the means by which the mind is strengthened and kindled to move from signs to things – *ep.* 55.9.21; *doc. Chr.* 2.6.7; *en.Ps.* 38.1; 138.31;146.12; 146.15; 149.14; *s.* 341.22. Conybeare (2012a) likewise comments on Augustine's own deliberately rude and crude language in the Confessions, to the same end: 'the emphasis on language as stumbling block – repeated sounds in studied lack of euphony, juxtapositions of consonants inviting hiatus or elision, resistance to rhythmical clausulae' (158). 'Words are used simultaneously to indicate possibility (the possibility of endless extension of meaning) and impossibility – the utter inadequacy of language before God. God must always be praised, even though the human tongue is wholly insufficient to praise him' (164).

[37] *en.Ps.* 137.2.

[38] *en.Ps.* 137.2.

[39] *en.Ps.* 125.5 137.2; 125.6: 'There, within you, is the mouth that will be filled with your joy, even when you are silent: for when you are silent but joyful your mouth is shouting to God.'

Lord himself taught that it was with such a voice that prayer should be made behind the closed doors of one's bedroom, that is to say, in the recesses of the heart, without any noise.[40]

Thus, when we truly pray, we bypass words in order to 'communicate' with God and be 'heard' by Him directly, inwardly and intuitively, inspired by the love and joy of God's presence. This is revealed above all in our faith in the sacrificial death of the Son for our sins and in the gift of the Holy Spirit, which is shed abroad in our hearts. As Augustine observes: 'A person of interior life (*homo interior*), one in whom Christ has begun to dwell through faith, must cry to the Lord with his own true voice, not with the noise of the lips but with the affection of the heart (*non in strepitu labiorum, sed in affectu cordis*).'[41]

More often than not, Augustine describes this inward, silent cry simply as a song: the 'song of the heart' or the 'new song'. Like prayer, he urges that this song should be unceasing, the perpetual, silent 'voice of our inner being', which continues to praise God, even when our vocal singing of hymns is over: 'When you come to church to join others in singing a hymn, your voice must chant (*sonat uox tua*) the praises of God. When you have sung as long as your strength allows, you go home; but then let your soul go on caroling [sounding] (*sonet anima tua*) the praises of God.'[42]

---

[40]*en.Ps.* 3.4; cf. 102.2; 125.6 God's voice, indeed God's singing, is heard in a similar way: *en.Ps.* 42.7: 'The soul is troubled by the imminence of death owing to its familiarity with the present world. But then it bends its ear to the inner voice of God, and hears within itself the song of reason. In our silence something sounds softly to us from above, reaching not our ears but our minds. Any who hear that music are so disenchanted with material noise (*strepitum corporalem*) that the whole of human life seems to them like a confused uproar, which stops them hearing another sound that is delightful, a sound like no other and beyond description.'

[41]Ibid. 141.2 Cf *s.* 341.16 where Augustine refers to the 'inexpressible voice of the heart (*ineffabili cordis uoce*)'. Origen makes a similar observation: 'Even if you do not know how you can give thanks to God in a worthy manner, you should still exult with the clear voice of a singing heart which soars above the signs of doubtful letters and express the mysterious and inexpressible despite the confusion of interpretations. If you soar above the sounds of words, if you keep within you the proclamation made with the mouth, if you can sing praise to God with just the spirit, your spirit, which does not know how to express its movements in words, because the word in you cannot carry the inexpressive and divine meaning of the Spirit – then you are singing to God', Comm. In Ps. Frag. 80.1 cited by King (2005) 146.

[42]*en.Ps.* 102.2 Cf *ep.* 140.

As the voice of faith, inspired by the indwelling of Christ and the grace of the Holy Spirit, it is a 'new song': the song, not of the Old Testament but of the New, not of the old man but the new man, not temporal but eternal, not motivated by sinful cupidity but by grace-filled love.[43] Above all, the new song is a song of freedom and love, not of slavery and fear: 'What, after all, has a new song got, but a new love? Singing is what a lover does. The voice of this singer indicates the fervor of a holy love (*Cantare amantis est. Vox huius cantoris, fervor sancti amoris*).'[44] This is not least because the 'new song' is in fact the song of God praising Himself through us. In the course of introducing a sermon on Psalm 144, Augustine observes that by giving us the Psalms and filling us inwardly with the Holy Spirit, God has graciously given us the means by which to praise Him, to delight in Him and to love Him:

> Knowing that it is good for us to love him, God has made himself lovable by praising himself, and in making himself lovable he has our good at heart. He therefore stirs up our hearts to praise him, and he has filled his servants with his own Spirit, to enable them to offer him praise. And if it is his own Spirit, present in his servants, who is praising him, what else can we conclude but that God is praising himself?.[45]

When he asks in another sermon on the Psalms whether we can do anything of our free will, rather than of necessity, the obvious answer therefore is: 'Yes, we certainly can. We find it when we praise God out of love for him. You act freely when you love what you praise, giving him glory not under compulsion but because you delight to praise him.'[46] Thus, in the act of praise, inspired by the love of God which is shed abroad in our hearts by the Holy Spirit, we are doing something which enables us to break free of the constraints of fallen necessity, ignorance and sin and which liberates us to do what we were created to do: to love and praise our Creator.

But what is this praise? Is it simply the silent shouting of the affections of the heart at prayer, the voice of the inner man which

---

[43]*en.Ps.* 32.ii.8; 66.6; 95.2; 136.13–17; 149.1–3; *s.* 33.1.
[44]*s.* 336.1.
[45]*en.Ps.* 144.1.
[46]Ibid. 134.11.

is heard by God without sound or words? Are 'praise' and 'song' simply mute analogies to illustrate what is, in effect, the voiceless, speechless movement of grace, which is given by God and which, in delight and love, returns us to Him? They are, of course, partly that.

An ethics of music: Singing with mouths, hearts and lives

But when the movement of the affections overflows; when the heart, like a pregnant woman on the point of giving birth, must bring forth what she has conceived[47]; when the fullness of love spills over in ineffable delight; and when the voice of the inner man can no longer keep silence, then they erupt in full-throated, resonant waves of rhythmic, wordless sound: the sound of jubilation. When words fail before the inexpressible goodness of God and we cannot remain silent, then, Augustine suggests, love finds a voice in shouts of joy:

> Words fail us, but love does not ... when we cannot articulate our thoughts, we must shout for joy. God is good, but what kind of good he is, who can tell? We cannot put it into words, but we are not allowed to remain silent. This is our problem: we cannot find words, but our sheer joy does not permit us to be silent; so let us neither speak nor hold our tongues. But what are we to do, if we can neither speak nor keep silence? Let us shout for joy. *Let us shout for joy to God, our salvation; shout with joy to God, all the earth* (Ps. 94.1; 99.1). What does that mean: *Shout for joy?* Give vent to the inarticulate expression of your joys, belch out (*eructate*) all your happiness to him. What kind of belching will there be after the final feasting, if even now after a modest meal our souls are so deeply affected?[48]

Before we examine the *jubilus* in more detail we should note that, in a very real sense, Augustine understands the whole of Christian

---

[47]Ibid. 137.4 'Our heart is pregnant, on the point of giving birth, and searching for a place to bring forth its adoration' Cf 32.ii.8; 65.2 'the sound of a heart labouring to bring forth into its voice its happiness over what it has conceived'.
[48]*en.Ps.* 102.8; Cf 134.3; 146.11.

life as a song of praise and rejoicing in response to the ineffable goodness of the Creator. We sing, not only with our voices, but with our minds and good works;[49] not only with our mouths, but with our hearts and lives.[50] In making this point Augustine is drawing attention to the fundamental fact, which shaped all philosophy and religion, that what we say and what we do are as inextricably linked as the body and soul; that the movement of one inevitably affects the other and is revealed in the other and that we cannot rejoice in God on the one hand and lead a sinful life on the other: 'What is the use of singing a hymn with your tongue, if your life breaths sacrilege?'.[51] This is partly a reflection on the basic truth that ontology is inseparable from psychology and ethics. When expressed in terms of music or song, it is as clear a statement as one could look for of the ontology, psychology and ethics which we argued structured Augustine's theological reflection on music from the very beginning: the whole of created reality, including ourselves, is a song, a *carmen universitatis*, composed and played by the divine Creator; everything we say, think and do – our voices, minds and lives – are formed and reformed by this music and our response to it. Our songs, thoughts and actions are all ways of expressing the inexpressible love and joy which God's music inspires within us so that like our songs, our lives become hymns of praise.[52]

In a number of the homilies on the Psalms Augustine – always fond of allegorizing the musical instruments which appear in the Psalter – likens our lives and actions to an instrument with which we accompany our singing so that together they praise God:

It is the same for you if, when you sing 'Alleluia' you also hand out bread to the hungry, clothe the naked, and welcome the traveler; then it is not only your voice that makes a sweet sound but your hands too are joining in, because your deeds are in tune with your words (*non sola uox sonat, sed et manus consonat, quia uerbis facta concordant*). You took up a musical

---

[49]*en.Ps.* 149.1.
[50]*en.Ps.* 149.6.
[51]Ibid. 102.28 Cf 132.5.
[52]Ibid. 126.1.

instrument (*organum*), and your fingers are in accord with your tongue.[53]

We should note that jubilation is a very particular sort of song: it is not a song which expresses lament and loss in wailing or groans (for the latter is a 'song of the flesh' not a 'song of the heart');[54] nor is it a song which expresses desire and longing in sighs and sobs. Neither is it the well-tempered, metrical feet of the verse Augustine carefully measured according to the art of music in *De musica*; nor is it a simple Christian hymn, written in memorable, easily performed iambic dimeter, such as Ambrose's congregation sang in Milan. Like its less articulate counterparts, which arise from the spontaneous, involuntary expression of overflowing emotion, jubilation is a wordless sound (*vox confusa*) rather than articulate speech (*vox articulata*), and like its more articulate counterparts, jubilation expresses the unknowable mysteries of God's gracious creation, providence, incarnation, redemption and sanctification. In jubilation, then, there are no words, no metre, no verses, no refrains – just sound: a voice bursting forth in praise and exaltation, a cry of pure joy expressing the riches of God's grace.

As far as I am aware it is only in the context of commenting on the Psalms that Augustine is prompted to reflect on the nature of jubilation, to explain it and to encourage his congregation to voice it. The obvious reason is the psalmists' own frequent call to 'rejoice', to 'shout for joy' to 'make a joyful noise' and to 'offer a sacrifice of joy': 'blessed are the people that knows how to shout for joy';[55] 'Make a joyful noise for the God of Jacob';[56] 'I have travelled round and now I have offered in his tent a sacrifice of great joy'.[57]

Less obvious is the fact that, although the Psalms were the hymn book of the Church, they were, in reality, a collection of songs or poems in translation. The original Hebrew had been translated into Greek or Latin and in the process a good deal of the rhythms of Hebrew parallelism had been lost in translation in order to preserve

---

[53]Ibid. 149.8. Cf 146.2; *s.* 256.1 Where he also comments in relation to the 'alleluia': 'so let us praise the Lord.... with our lives and our tongues, with hearts and mouths, with our voices and our behaviour'.
[54]Ibid. 37.13.
[55]*en.Ps.* 88.16 on Psa. 88.16.
[56]*en.Ps.* 80.3 on Psa. 80.2.
[57]*en.Ps.* 26.1.6 Cf 26.ii.12 on Psa. 26.6.

the sense.[58] Like Ambrose's hymns, we simply don't know how the Psalms were sung by early Christians; all that we have is abundant evidence (which we noted above) for their ubiquity and popularity, both inside and outside the context of the liturgy. That they were sung is beyond doubt, that they were sung without any instrumental accompaniment (at least in Church) is also beyond question, and that they were sung responsorially is also pretty certain,[59] but apart from that we can only guess. There are tantalizing hints in Athanasius's *Letter to Marcellinus* as to the manner and sound of their performance. Athanasius (the fourth-century bishop of Alexandria) explains that we sing, rather than say the Psalms, because 'it is fitting for the Divine Scripture to praise God not in compressed speech alone, but also in the voice that is richly broadened ... of this kind are the psalms, odes and songs. For thus will it be preserved that men love God with their whole strength and power'.[60] Is this a reflection on the effect of translation as well as the effect of singing? Had the Psalms been freed up to allow the heart's affections to be voiced, not in a particular poetic form but in pure sound, which comprehended their force and power? Does he even have in mind something like the *jubilus* or shout of joy, which broke through the measured words of the Psalm in a cry of inexpressible gladness and rejoicing?

We must also take account of the fact that whatever form early Christian singing took and whatever it sounded like, it was not written down but was known and performed by memory, based on imitation, repetition and formulaic oral transmission.[61] This meant that, to a much greater degree than later fixed, scripted, notated music, it was open to improvisation and allowed freedom for spontaneous jubilation.

---

[58]*ep.* 101.4 'I have not written anything on the metre found in the verses of David. For the translator from the Hebrew language, which I do not know, was not able also to indicate the metre for fear that the demands of the metre would force him to depart from the truth in his translation more than the sense of the verses permitted. I believe those who know that language well that those verses have a definite metre. For that holy man loved religious music and kindles our love for such studies more than any other author.'
[59]The Psalm was sung or read by a lector between the OT and NT lessons at the Eucharist, and at Vespers and Matins; Augustine often refers to a refrain sung by the congregation. For references, see WSA III/15, 16 n.22.
[60]Athanasius *Letter to Marcellinus* 28–29 (Gregg, 124–125).
[61]Potter and Sorrell (2012) 42f.

A theology of music

In addition to prompts from the psalmist, Augustine's own explanation of why we find ourselves shouting for joy in the midst of a song is one we should attend to most carefully. We jubilate, he suggests, for two main reasons and they are the same as the ones which we have already seen prompt the heart to silent, inexpressible prayer: we jubilate firstly in response to the overwhelming gifts of God's grace, and secondly in response to His ineffable presence and transcendence. Both His grace and His majesty, as it were, render us speechless; both move us to praise; both propel song to take flight in wordless shouts of joy.

The gifts of God's grace comprehend, for Augustine, the whole economy of salvation. More often than not, passages describing the *jubilus* follow a consideration of the psalmist's account of God's gracious creation, providence, redemption and sanctification of his people. In passages which closely echo the more well-known account in *Confessions* book 10 (which we touched upon), in which he describes his ascent from creation, through the senses, the soul, the mind and memory, and then above the memory to God, who at once transcends it and deigns to dwell in it, Augustine traces similar ascents of the soul across the *Enarrationes in Psalmos*.[62] When he gazed upon creation and wondered at its beauty in the *Confessions* he received the response: '"We are not God" and "He made us".' 'My questioning', he observes, 'was my attentive spirit, and their reply, their beauty (*interrogatio mea intentio mea et responsio eorum species eorum*)'.[63] In the *Enarrationes*, gazing is transposed into hearing: his question is his listening to creation; its answer is its song: 'the dumb earth sings with the voice of its beauty (*uox quaedam est mutae terrae, species terrae*)',[64] the psalmist sings, 'shout with joy to the Lord, all the earth'.[65] Although the earth's song may be a metaphorical one, it is also, as we saw in Chapter 1, an ontological one, and it resounds in Augustine's emphatically vocal response to it: in the eruption of a wordless shout of joy. The fact that the earth's beauty 'sings' is, of course, due to its creation by

---

[62]notably *en.Ps.* 26.ii.12; 41. 2–10; 99.5; 134.4; 144.6–10.
[63]*conf.* 10.7.9.
[64]*en.Ps.* 144.13.
[65]Ibid. 99.2–3.

God, His providential ordering of it and the cosmic harmony that holds everything in unity.[66] God, the Creator, Augustine affirms in Psalm 99, is 'present everywhere, and everywhere totally' (99.5). But he is clearly struggling to find words to describe the theological ontology on which the song of jubilation is based: the best he can do, apart from the language of omnipresence, is – as so often – to cite Scripture: 'His Wisdom reaches powerfully from end to end, disposing all things sweetly' (Wisdom 8.1) .... 'for in him we live and move and have our being' (Acts 17:28) ... 'God's invisible reality is contemplated through things that are created' (Romans 1:20). Alternatively, he offers an artistic analogy:

> Let your mind roam round the whole creation: from all sides creation will cry to you 'God made me'. Whatever delights you in art points you to the artist and all the more so if you go round the whole created order: gazing on it fills you with longing to praise its maker. ... Everything everywhere shouts back to you the name of the Creator, and the varied beauties of created things are a chorus [voice] of praise to him (*et ipsae species creaturarum, uoces sunt quaedam creatorem laudantium*).[67]

In *epistle* 166 to Jerome, the 'art' is identified with the silent, measured, harmonious music of the providential order of creation and human life, and the 'artist' with God, its composer. 'If we did perceive it', Augustine observes,

> we would be comforted by an ineffable delight.[68] For it was not said in vain of God that ... *He produces the world in harmony* (*qui perfert numerose saeculum*) (Is 40:26 LXX). Hence the generosity of God has granted music, that is, a knowledge or perception of harmony [rhythmic measure] (*scientia sensusue bene modulandi*),[69] even to mortals who have rational souls in

---

[66]Ibid. 99.5 Cf *ciu.* 11.4 'The very order, changes and movements in the universe, the very beauty of form in all that is visible, proclaim, however silently, both that the world was created and also that its Creator could be none other than God whose greatness and beauty are both ineffable and invisible.'

[67]Ibid. 26.12 Cf; 26.ii.8; 134.5.

[68]*ep.* 166.13.

[69]The reader will recall that this is precisely how Augustine defined music at the beginning of *De musica: musica est scientia bene modulandi.*

order to call their attention to something important. A human artist composing a song knows what length to give to what sounds in order that a melody may emerge and dissipate as subsequent sounds take the place of earlier ones. Hence, how much more does God-whose wisdom, by which he made all things, is preferable to all the arts – not allow any stretches of time in natures that are born and die, which are like syllables and words in relation to the parts of this age, to pass faster or slower in this marvelous song (*mirabili cantico*), as it were, of passing things, than the measure that he foreknew and predetermined demands! Since I would also say this of the leaf of a tree and of the number of our hairs, how much more do I say this of the birth and death of a human being, whose temporal life does not extend shorter or longer than God, who gives order to the times (*dispositor temporum*), knows harmonizes with the melody of the universe(*nouit uniuersitatis moderamini consonare*).[70]

Creation, of course, also includes human beings, and the fact that Augustine can contemplate creation, hear it and delight in it, and then sing in praise of its Creator is, in turn, due to *his* creation by God, who also sings through Him, inspiring His love and delight: 'Whatever instrument God's voice employs, God's voice it is still. Nothing but his own voice sounds sweetly in his ears. When we speak we delight him, as long as he speaks through us.'[71]

'The heart's cry of joy is its understanding' (*en.Ps.* 99.3)

'Jubilation is a shout of joy; it indicates that the heart is bringing forth what defies speech. To whom, then, is this jubilation more

---

[70]*ep.* 166.13 Cf *en.Ps.* 9.7 where, as we saw, Augustine refers to a 'verse in the mind' which is eternal and unchangeable, and a 'verse in the voice' which is temporal and mutable (it 'sounds in the air and is gone'). The former regulates the latter, as God orders everything by his providence.
[71]*en.Ps.* 99.1 Cf 144.7.

fittingly offered than to God who surpasses all utterance (*Et quem decet ista jubilatio, nisi ineffabilem Deum*)?' (*en.Ps.* 32.ii.8).[72] Augustine insists that it is only when the song of praise which human beings offer back to the Creator breaks into wordless joy that we be truly said to 'understand' God. Citing Psalm 88.16, 'Blessed the people that understands how to shout with joy', he observes that 'the heart's cry of joy is its understanding'.[73] What he means by this extraordinary claim – 'the heart's cry of joy is its understanding' – is, I think, that it is only when we become aware that God cannot be captured by words but can only be expressed in spontaneous, involuntary shouts of joy, that we truly 'understand' Him. In other words, that God is 'understood', not intellectually but in the 'cry of the heart', in the wordless, jubilant sound of praise, not rationally but affectively. Above all, Augustine reminds his congregation that if we want to say what God is, the only answer is love: He is 'known' in the love which inspires our singing, the love which is expressed in the song and which thereby reforms His likeness in us so that we can recognize Him, who is Love, and truly rejoice in His unknowable and ineffable transcendence in wordless cries of joy.

To know God, then, is to know that he can never be known, but only praised – in the wordless sound of jubilation:

'if you are like him, you will leap for joy. As you begin to resemble him and draw near, and begin to be keenly aware of God, charity will grow in you; and since charity is also God, you will be conscious of the reality you tried to talk about, though you did not truly speak of it at all. Before you became so vividly aware of Him you thought yourself qualified to speak about God; but now you begin to feel what He is, and you realize that what you perceive is something that cannot be spoken. But if you have discovered that the reality you encounter is beyond utterance, will you therefore fall silent and not praise Him? Will you be struck dumb and cease to praise God, and no longer give thanks to Him who has willed to

---

[72]*Bibliothèque Augustinienne* 11.2 note complémentaire 5.3 (*l'ineffabilité divine*) for references to God's ineffability in Augustine's other works, Neoplatonic background, secondary literature on negative theology and some interesting comments on how Augustine diverges from the emphasis on silence before the unknowable God, which is so characteristic of Porphyry, and instead emphasizes praise and jubilation.
[73]Ibid. 99.3.

make Himself known to you? Listen to the Psalm: 'Shout with joy to the Lord, all the earth (*Jubilate Domino omnis terra*).'[74]

Interestingly, Augustine relates our speechlessness before God, as well as our ability to nevertheless praise Him in shouts of joy, to the Creator Word and the Incarnate Word respectively:

'He alone is inexpressible (*ineffabilis*), he who spoke and all things were made. He spoke, and we came to be, but we have no power to utter him. The Word in whom we were spoken is His Son, and to enable us weaklings to utter him in some degree, the Word became weak. We can shout in exultation (*Jubilationem*) over the Word, but we can find no words to articulate the Word (*uerbum pro uerbo non possumus*). 'Shout with joy to the Lord, all the earth.'[75]

So, although we cannot articulate God's Word we *can* at least sing to Him; words will not suffice, but the sound of the *vox confusa* will! As Augustine tells his congregation, what they need to know, above all else – for therein lies their ultimate happiness or blessedness – is 'how to rejoice in something you cannot put into words'. Quoting Psalm 88: 16 again, 'blessed the people that knows how to shout with joy', he comments,

> O blessed people, do you think you apprehend what shouting for joy is? You cannot be blessed unless you do understand it .... For your joy does not spring from yourself; rather let anyone who would glory, glory in the Lord ... So great is his grace that no tongue is fit to express it. Grasp this, and you have understood about shouting for joy ... see if it is not delight in grace, delight in God.[76]

Similarly, although God's goodness exceeds anything that the heart or mind can conceive and 'we lack the capacity to contemplate Him in Himself', Augustine urges his congregation not to fall silent but rather to praise Him for His works, which they *can* contemplate, and most especially for the gift of His Son, the mediator, through whom they can taste of God's sweetness and receive the bread of

---

[74]Ibid. 99.6 Cf *en.Ps.* 26.i.6.
[75]Ibid. 99.6; Cf 134.5.
[76]Ibid. 88.16–17 Cf. Jerome on Psalm 32 (PL 26,970) *Jubilus dicitur, quod nec uerbis, nec syllabis nec litteris nec uoce potest erumpere aut comprehendere quantum homo Deum debeat laudare.*

angels: '*Sing psalms to his name*, then, *because he is sweet*. If you have tasted, sing psalms; if you have tasted and discovered how sweet the Lord is, sing psalms; if you relish what you have tasted, praise him.'[77]

As we have observed – though it hardly needs to be said – Augustine's language in these Psalms is not that of rational cognition, for he is persuaded that this is impossible and beyond our power; it is, rather, the language of affective cognition, in which we become aware of God's unknowable and ineffable presence through delight and love. As he observes on Psalm 32.8, 'Sing him a new song', we are like those who find themselves having to sing before a master musician but are at a complete loss, having had no instruction in the art of singing (*sine aliqua instructione musicae artis cantare*), and therefore no idea how to do it or what to sing, in order not to offend, but to please, Him. Thankfully, he comments, God has given us a 'technique for singing (*modum cantandi*)'.[78] It is not a matter of words – as if any words could please God – but rather a matter of jubilation:

A person who is shouting with gladness does not bother to articulate words. The shout is a wordless sound of joy; it is the cry of a mind expanded with gladness, expressing its feelings as best it can rather than comprehending the sense (*exprimentis affectum, non sensum comprehendentis*). When someone is exulting and happy he passes beyond words that can be spoken and understood, and bursts forth into a wordless cry of exultation. Such a person is clearly rejoicing vocally, but he is so full of intense joy that he is unable to explain what makes him happy.[79]

By now the patient reader might well be wondering: but is this really music? Is the *jubilus* really a song and not just a shout? In fact, in Augustine's mind, the *jubilus* and song are synonymous: jubilation is, for him, the definition of song: 'singing belongs to joy

[77]Ibid. 134.5.
[78]This could, of course, also refer to a harmonic mode, as well as a 'mode' or technique of singing.
[79]Ibid. 99.4 Cf 26.ii.12; 46.7; 80.3.

(*psallere autem ad gaudium pertinet*)'.[80] Reflecting on the distinction
between a Psalm and a song, Augustine tentatively suggests that
whereas 'song may mean only joy, those which are sung to the
accompaniment of the psaltery are called psalms'.[81] It may well be
that the distinction he has in mind is between secular and sacred
song: all song is an expression of joy, but Psalms are sacred songs
which were traditionally accompanied by an instrument (and
so originate in an intertwining of the psalmist's articulate voice
with the psaltery's confused voice). As Augustine observes, this is
certainly what David did: 'The historical books tell us that David
the prophet used the psaltery as part of a great mystery.'[82] But this
was not the practice of the early Church which, as we have noted,
generally forbade the use of musical instruments in worship (at
least in Church).[83] Perhaps, then, this distinction is a historical
one; Psalms were in origin accompanied sacred songs; songs are
simply expressions of joy. Having raised the question Augustine
ducks the task of resolving it: 'Here is not the place to examine
this question, because it requires a protracted investigation and a
lengthy discussion.' I propose to duck it for the same reasons, as I
am not aware that he ever returned to it. What is important for our
purposes is that when he mentions jubilation he most definitely has
singing in mind, not just an inarticulate shout; indeed, he thinks
that jubilation (rejoicing, happiness) is the defining characteristic of
song. As he is so often prompted to comment when preaching on a
Psalm: '"A song of praise, for David himself." Now the designation
"song of praise," connotes both cheerfulness, since this is a song,
and devotion, since it expresses praise. ... Let us praise him, and
sing as we do so; let us praise him, I mean, cheerfully and with
joy.'[84]

Augustine, then, acknowledges that the role of song – secular as
well as sacred – is to celebrate happiness, to articulate cheerfulness
and give voice to joy. When he wants to explain the *jubilus* to his
congregation he therefore deploys strikingly earthy and worldly

---

[80]Ibid. 7.19.
[81]Ibid. 4.1.
[82]Ibid. 4.1.
[83]Shirt (2015).
[84]Ibid. 94.1.

examples: they know what the *jubilus* is because they have heard in everyday life:

> *Let us shout for joy to God, our salvation.* What is shouting for joy (*jubilare*)? When we cannot express our joy in words, and yet we want to use our voices to give proof of what we have conceived within but cannot articulate, that is shouting for joy. Consider beloved ones, how people sing songs (*cantilenis*) when they are making merry, vying with each other in celebrating worldly happiness. You know how sometimes, in between songs with words, the singers seem to overflow with a joy that the tongue is inadequate to express verbally; you know how then they let out wild whoops to give utterance to a gladness of spirit (*quemadmodum jubilent, ut per illam uocem indicetur animi affectus*), since they are unable to put into words what the heart has conceived. Well then, if they shout for joy over earthy happiness, ought not we to shout for joy over heavenly happiness, which certainly cannot be spelled out in words?[85]

Elsewhere Augustine gives the example of people shouting for joy at the circus,[86] at harvest, in the vineyard, fruit-picking or when engaged in any other vigorous occupation:[87] 'They begin by caroling their joy in words, but after a while they seem to be so full of gladness that they find words no longer adequate to express it, so they abandon distinct syllables and words, and resort to a single cry of jubilant happiness (*sonum jubilationis*).'[88]

Like Monnica's recitation of the closing lines of Ambrose's *Deus Creator Omnium* in *De beata uita*, or the singing of Ambrose's hymns by his congregation, the *jubilus* is a democratic song which does not require education, literacy or any musical expertise but simply the compulsion to sing and, in a Christian context, to thereby express the ineffable mysteries of the faith by giving sound to them.

---

[85]Ibid. 94.3.
[86]Ibid. 80.3.
[87]Ibid. 32.ii.8; 99.4.
[88]Ibid. 32.ii.8; 99.4 Is this laughter?

Songs without words

We should note that the *jubilus* arises *from within* song and that it is only when the words of the song falter and fail that it breaks forth into worldless sound.[89] But is the *jubilus* itself a song? We have discovered that it is a shout, a cry, a spontaneous eruption of sound which resembles nothing more than a belch, but is it song? Augustine seems to think so: we have seen that for him it is the divinely given technique for singing (*modum cantandi*), which God has provided precisely for those occasions when we have neither the skill nor the words to express what fills our hearts to overflowing. But if it is song, what sort of song is it? Theologians from Amalar, in the ninth century, onwards, seem to have instinctively related the *jubilus* to the sinuous, seductive, melismatic chant which was used to draw out the final syllable/vowel of the Alleluia into virtually wordless, seemingly unending, ecstatically rising and falling praise. In the singing of the Alleluia the syllables of the word were subsumed in the – sometimes notated, sometimes improvised – waves of sound; sound gave the word movement, space and the ability to take on many different guises and feelings, affording the hearer space to recollect, follow and meditate; in other words sound took over from words to express the unknowable mystery of God and to praise His ineffable greatness.[90]

Perhaps the instincts of medieval theologians were right, but Augustine's description of the *jubilus* is, as we have seen, rather

---

[89]Ibid 32.ii.8 (Cf 99.4). A point made by Isaac Harrison Louth ('*Ecce cano – Look, I sing!* Translating between Sound, Sign and Script in Anglo-Saxon Winchester' unpublished paper). Commenting on this passage he writes, 'Augustine writes that singers in jubilation turn away (*auertunt*) from the syllables of words (*syllabis uerborum*) towards sound (*sonum jubilationis*) but notes that the very joy (*laetitia*) which motivates them springs in the first place from their exulting (*exsultare*) in the words of the songs (*in uerbis canticorum*).' He observes: 'There is a way in which jubilant sound burst forth from the text and, at the same time, works itself free of the text.'

[90]Treitler (2003); Zorzi (2002) 349. Augustine does not appear to make this identification, however, despite the obvious parallels. McKinnon (1996) 212, is emphatic: 'I should like to assert categorically that the patristic references to this musical phenomenon have nothing to do with the Alleluia of the Mass, nor, for that matter, with any other genre of ecclesiastical song.' See Bernard of Clairvaux *Sermon 67, On the Song of Songs* (Kalamazoo MI: Cistercian Publications, 3–16), for a very similar account of affective jubilation (including belching).

more earthy: it arises from labour – the pregnant woman, the worker in the vineyard, the peasant gathering grapes or taking in the harvest.[91] It arises from the attempt to contain and confine what the singer knows and feels in measured verse and articulate words. It arises from the effort to somehow express the immensity and wondrous, awe-inspiring generosity of God's gifts. It arises from the struggle to articulate what is ineffable – and then, suddenly, we are set free: the *jubilus* escapes, explodes – and is brought forth in wordless cries, finally expressing the unknowable, ineffable riches of God's grace and majesty by returning them to Him in joy, love and praise. It is difficult to think of a modern musical analogy to capture this: scat singing – the random, exuberant, expressive sound which uses the whole range and timbre of the voice in jazz singing; yodelling or folk-singing – where the voice rises and falls in waves – sometimes shouts – of wordless sound;[92] the waves of clashing voices in Ethiopian liturgical singing; the melismatic improvisations of Orthodox chant; the extemporary, improvised ornaments, cadenzas and variations of classical, instrumental and vocal music; the non-verbal, inspired utterances of glossolalia or speaking in tongues[93] are perhaps the closest we can come to

---

[91]McKinnon (1996) 215–216 notes that the *jubilus* most commonly appears in classical literature in an agrarian context but that it is a translation of the Greek (LXX) 'alalagmos', which, in contrast, has military connotations and is always used in this sense in Greek commentaries on the Psalms. He cites Hilary of Poitiers, who makes this difference clear in *Homilies on the Psalms* 45.3 (MECL 124–125): 'According to the conventions of our language we give the name *jubilus* to the sound of a pastoral and rustic voice ... But among the Greeks the term *alalagmos* means the cry of an army in battle.' The *celeuma*, or the rhythmic pattern of shouts (usually accompanied by the aulos), which sailors used to encourage their work by setting the pace for the oarsmen, is another example of wordless music which is related to heavy labour. It is one which Augustine is aware of, but he does not mention it in relation to the *jubilus*. On the *celeuma*, see Sheerin (1982) who notes that early medieval Christians related it to the Alleluia.
[92]McKinnon (1996) 215 notes that *jubilus* derives from the root *io*, which serves as an exclamation in various languages, no doubt because of its sound – as in the 'modern "Yo," the Alpine yodel and the cries of the Volga boatmen'.
[93]Werner (1959) 154 observes that 'when the spontaneous outpourings of glossolaly and prophetic-mystic hymns threatened to upset the unity of Christianity as well as the order of its worship, the psalms, with their ancient, well-established textual and musical tradition, served as regulators and teachers in the turbulent spiritual upheavals that preceded the fourth and fifth centuries. The last and most precious remnant of that period of spontaneity is probably the jubilus, the musical, wordless-ecstatic hymn, the element of glossolaly converted to organized, melismatic psalmody'.

guessing what the *jubilus* must have sounded like. As in Augustine's
analogies, in these examples, too, the *jubilus* arises from within; it
grows out of, emerges and explodes from the confines of singing
in words (or scripted notation) into the freedom of singing in
spontaneous, improvised sound.[94] The *jubilus*, then, is the sort of
song that liberates us from the slavery of words and enables us –
at least momentarily – to act freely and to be united with God in
praise and rejoicing.

When we examined the ascent at Ostia in the previous chapter
we suggested that it might henceforth be known, not as the 'vision
at Ostia' but as the 'praise at Ostia'. In common with the many
Neoplatonic-type ascents which Augustine traces, this one ends
in a moment which, if it could become permanent, would be
indistinguishable from the life to come.[95] Words elude Augustine
when he tries to describe what is attained at the height of these
ascents: it is a 'flash of one tremulous glance (*in ictu trepidantis
aspectus*)',[96] 'the utmost leap of our hearts ... a flash of thought
... a moment of knowledge (*toto ictu cordis ... rapida cogitatione
... momentum intelligentiae*)',[97] an overwhelming sense of God's
voice, touch, taste and smell.[98] It is this moment, I think, which
the *jubilus* expresses, a moment when happiness or blessedness is
achieved in unreserved, unconstrained joy, love and delight in God's
gracious presence, captured, in this life, in fleeting song – for as
with all the ascents, the *jubilus* which we sing here must fall back
to the temporal, mutable succession of words which define our
earthly (fallen) existence. Nevertheless, it is a glimpse, a foretaste,
a proleptic revelation of the life to come, when we will praise God
eternally in wordless songs of endless joy: 'If this could last ... so
that this moment of knowledge – this passing moment that left us
aching for more – should there be life eternal, would not *Enter into
the joy of your Lord* (Mt. 25.21) be this, and this alone?'[99]

Augustine often reverts to the monastic life as a model and
foretaste of what the life to come will be like, and as the closest

[94]Ibid. 32.ii.8; 99.3–4.
[95]*conf.* 9.10.25.
[96]*conf.* 7.17.23.
[97]*conf.* 9.10.24–25.
[98]*conf.* 10.27.38.
[99]*conf.* 9.10.25.

we can come to it in this life; it consists of 'holy men whose lives
are given to hymnody and prayer and praise of God'.[100] But even
in the monastery, jubilation is not yet perfect; although a harbour
and refuge, the monastery is still open to the buffeting waves
of temptation.[101] The monks take delight in hope, rather than
attainment;[102] their confession is a mixture of confession of sin and
confession of praise,[103] groans and jubilation.[104] Only in the life to
come will the gates of the harbour be shut and they will attain
'perfect jubilation'.[105]

The *jubilus* is therefore a momentary glimpse of the life to come,
when we will be liberated from the constraints of sin, time and
mutability and be free to confess our endless love and delight in God
in joyful, unconstrained, unconfined songs of everlasting praise:
'Prayer [which is for those in need] will pass away, praise will take
over; weeping will pass away, joy will take its place';[106] 'endless love
of God will be expressed in endless praise'.[107] 'Once freed from the
narrow confinement of this corruptible state', Augustine therefore
observes, 'we shall dwell in God's house, and our whole life will be
nothing but praise of God'.[108]

However earthy the origins of jubilation are, then, its end is
most definitely spiritual – we might almost say, mystical. It captures
those moments of ecstasy – of being ravished, caught up, consumed
by the sweetness of God's grace and inflamed by His love, which
we fleetingly glimpse and taste in this life but which will be our
permanent state in the life to come. It also captures those moments
when words fall away before the unknowable and ineffable God –
as when Paul describes being 'taken up to the third heaven, where
he heard words beyond all utterance that no human may speak',[109]
or when Augustine and Monnica were momentarily caught up
into wordless, ecstatic rapture and then 'returned to the noise of

---

[100]*en.Ps.* 99.12.
[101]Ibid. 99.9 Cf 103.4.
[102]Ibid. 99.8.
[103]Ibid. 99.16.
[104]Ibid. 99.9.
[105]Ibid. 99. 8, 11.
[106]Ibid. 26.ii.14.
[107]Ibid. 99.11; 141.19; 144.5–6.
[108]Ibid. 141.19.
[109]Ibid. 37.12.

articulate speech, where a word has beginning and end'.[110] In the life to come, when words will no longer be necessary, we will praise God in never-ending, wordless song.

Sorabji observes that for Plotinus the love involved in mystical contemplation is an emotion which cannot involve judgement because judgement involves duality, and duality is, by definition, excluded by mystical union. Like the natural sense of hearing which instinctively takes delight in what is pleasing and harmonious without the need for rules of judgement, and which we discovered was Augustine's way of describing the love which God's grace sheds abroad in our hearts, so that we are inexorably moved to take delight in and participate in Him, so, I would like to suggest, in the life to come the *jubilus* will be an expression of love and praise by which we are united with God, through the love and praise He inspires within us for Himself. As Plotinus writes in one of the *Enneads* we are almost certain Augustine knew: 'This contemplation is intellect in love, when it goes out of its mind, drunk with nectar. Then it falls in love, made simple and transformed into happy feeling (*eupatheia*) by satiety,'[111] or as Augustine himself puts it, 'There we shall be still and see; we shall see and we shall love; we shall love and we shall praise.'[112] It is no coincidence, then, that Augustine often tends to use the metaphors of fire and drunkenness to describe the effect of music: they are at once uncontrollable and all-consuming.[113]

Following the psalmist, for whom the image of God's dwelling place signifies His holy and ineffable presence – in the tents of Israel, in the Temple, in His saints, in the heavenly Jerusalem – Augustine, too, is fond of expressing the gift of God's grace and love in terms of His indwelling.[114] He dwells in both the congregation of the

---

[110]*conf.* 9.10.24.

[111]*Ennead.* 6.7.35 Quoted by Sorabji (2000) 142.

[112]*ciu.* 22.30.

[113]Noted by Moorhead (2010) 87–89. As Polanyi (1958) 198, puts it, 'Proximity to God is not an observation, for it overwhelms the worshipper. An observer must be relatively detached from that which he observes, and religious experience transforms the worshipper. It stands in this respect closer to sensual abandon than to exact observation.'

[114]Fiedrowicz (WSA III/15) 63–64 comments on Psalm 83.5, 'Blessed are they who dwell in your house; they will praise you for ever and ever' that it 'runs through the whole of Augustine's expositions of the psalms like a refrain: he cites it twenty-one times'.

faithful below and in the assembly of the angels above; both are
His temple so that when we exult and glory in Him on earth our
praise joins us with that of the angels: 'When, therefore, our joy
springs ... from spiritual causes, and we are inspired to strike up
a song to God (*canticum Deo*) and sing to him in the presence of
the angels, this very concourse of angels is God's temple, and we
worship in it. The Church is both here below and on high.'[115] In
singing the Psalms Augustine tells his congregation that they are
joining themselves with the members of the body of Christ; they are
identifying themselves with those who exult and joy in hope, making
their voice their own voice. He effectively tells them to listen with
their eyes and see with their ears: 'Listen', he urges them, 'as if you
were looking at your own reflection in the mirror of the scriptures
(*in speculo Scripturarum*)[116] .... When in your exultant hope you
observe the likeness between yourself and other members of Christ,
the members who first sang these verses, you will be certain that
you are among his members, and you will sing them'.[117]

Whereas we are still on pilgrimage, singing and taking joy in
hope, Augustine observes, that those whose voices we join ourselves
with are those who have escaped this world, who have reached
their destination and are singing and exulting with Christ. 'Let us
sing the psalm together', he therefore tells his listeners, 'both the
saints who rejoice in the reality and we who join them in hope ...
longing to share that life which we do not have here but which we
shall never have unless here on earth we desired it'.[118] Singing the
Psalms therefore, we are united not only with those who originally
sang them, with those who now sing them in hope, but also with
those who eternally sing them in joy and exaltation in the life to
come: our singing joins us to a community or choir of singers which
stretches out before and after us; it catches us up into a universal
song and draws us towards its inspiration, source and end. Thus,
commenting on Psalm 136, Augustine observes that, like the
Israelites in Babylon, singing the Lord's song in a strange land, the

---

[115]*en.Ps.* 137.4.
[116]This very much echoes Athanasius's *Letter to Marcellinus* 12 'And it seems to me
that these words become like a mirror to the person singing them, so that he might
perceive himself and the emotions of his soul, and thus affected, he might recite
them.'
[117]*en.Ps.* 123.3.
[118]*en.Ps.* 123.3.

song of the faithful in this world is not a foreign, barbaric song picked up in captivity but rather their own native song, the one that springs naturally from the heart of every Christian in exile from their homeland: 'The song of Jerusalem is our own language,' he comments.[119] And when their exile and pilgrimage is ended, they will not cease to sing but will offer God an eternal *jubilus*: '*They shall exult for ever and ever and you will dwell in them* (5.12). That, then, will be eternal rejoicing, when the just are the temple of God, and He, dwelling in them, will be their joy.'[120] Thus, although we sing 'Alleluiah' in our fallen state, full of anxiety and care, still travelling amidst dangers and trials, we do so in the hope of the life to come, when we will sing unburdened of the tribulations and temptations that now assail us, with an unalloyed joy:

> Oh, what a happy *alleluia* there, how carefree, how safe from all opposition, where nobody will be an enemy, no one cease to be a friend! God praised there, and God praised here; here, though, by the anxious, there by the carefree; here by those who are going to die, there by those who are going to live forever; here in hope, there in hope realized; here on the way, there at home.[121]

At the beginning of this chapter we joined the noisy party of voices resounding in classical literature; at the end of it, we have discovered that, for the Christian, what is heard is ultimately the voice of God – or better, the singing of God – sounding in the harmonious song of His creation, providence and salvation. God's voice is a mellifluous voice, which inspires in the hearer an overwhelming delight and desire to hear more, for its sweetness is redolent of His unknowable and ineffable transcendence, which cannot be expressed in words but only in joyful rejoicing and praise. In this life, the melody is heard as fleetingly as a touch or glance; it sounds and passes away, leaving us with an aching longing and desire to hold it fast. When we do ultimately hear it in the life to come, we will discover that it is the echo of a never-ending party, one which does not pass away, but is a festival of eternal rejoicing and praise in the eternal and transcendent God, who has always sung, and will always continue

---

[119]*en.Ps.* 136.17.
[120]*en.Ps.* 5.16.
[121]*s.* 256. 3.

to sing, in and through us, uniting us with each other and with Himself, in joy and love.

In his homily on Psalm 41, *By the voice of exultation and praise, the sounds of one celebrating a festival*, Augustine describes the earthly member of the Church (the tent of God on pilgrimage in this world) who is drawn towards the melodious and delightful strains of music coming from the eternal house of God in the heavens. Just as the sound of singing and playing draws our attention to a house where a birthday or wedding is taking place, so we are drawn by the music of the angels' eternal praise to the unending party of heaven. He writes,

> He was drawn toward a kind of sweetness, an inward, secret pleasure that cannot be described, as though some musical instrument were sounding delightfully from God's house. As he still walked about in the tent he could hear this inner music; he was drawn to its sweet tones, following its melodies and distancing himself from the din of flesh and blood, until he found his way even to the house of God. He tells us about the road he took and the manner in which he was led, as though we had asked him, 'You admire the tent on earth, but how did you reach the secret precincts of God's house?' *By the voice of exultation and praise*, he says, *the sounds of one celebrating a festival* .... In God's home there is an everlasting party. What is celebrated there is not some occasion that passes; the choirs of angels keep eternal festival, for the eternally present face of God is joy never diminished. This is a feast day that does not open at dawn, or close at sundown. From that eternal, unfading festival melodious and delightful sound reaches the ears of the heart .... The sweet strains of that celebration are wafted into the ears of the one who walks in the tent and ponders the wonderful works of God in the redemption of believers, and they drag the deer toward the springs of water. [122]

---

[122]*en.Ps.* 41.9 Augustine often talks of catching the strains of a song coming from Zion – Cf 136.13.

BIBLIOGRAPHY

Texts

Abbreviations

AL   *Augustinus-Lexikon* Mayer, Cornelius Petrus, Karl Heinz Chelius, and Erich Feldmann (eds.) (Shwabe: Verlag, 1986–)

ACW   Ancient Christian Writers (New York, NY: Paulist)

CCL   Corpus Christianorum, Series Latina (Turnhout: Brepols)

CPG   Clavis Patrum Graecorum, M. Geerard (ed). 5 vols. (Turnhout: Brepols)

CSEL   Corpus Scriptorum Ecclesiasticorum Latinorum (Vienna: Tempsky)

FC   Fathers of the Church (Washington, DC: Catholic University of America)

LCC   Library of Christian Classics (London: SCM)

Loeb Loeb   Classical Library (Cambridge, MA: Harvard University Press and London: Heinemann)

NPNF   Nicene and Post-Nicene Fathers, Series 1–2

PG   Patrologia Graeca, ed. J.-P. Migne

PL   Patrologia Latina, ed. J.-P. Migne

SC   Sources Chrétiennes (Paris: Cerf)

WSA   The Works of Saint Augustine: A Translation for the 21st Century John E. Rotelle (ed.) (Hyde Park, NY: New City Press)

The Revised Standard Version of the Bible has been used for quotations.

Aristides Quintilianus

On Music

On Music in Barker 1984: Thomas J. Mathiesen, *Aristides Quintilianus, On Music.* Translation with introduction, commentary and annotations. Music Theory Translation Series. (New Haven and London: Yale University Press, 1983)

Athanasius

To Marcellinus, on the Psalms

Athanasius: The Life of Antony and the Letter to Marcellinus, tr. R.C. Gregg, Classics of Western Spirituality (Mahwah, NJ: Paulist, 1980)
PG 27.11–46

Augustine

c.Acad. = *Against the Academics*
WSA 1.3
Contra Academicos CCL 29

b. uita = On the Happy Life
FC 1
De beata uita CSEL 63

cat. rud. = *On Teaching the Uninstructed*
WSA I.10 (*On Instructing Beginners in the Faith*)
De catechizandis rudibus CCL 46

ciu. = City of God
Bettenson (1972)
De ciuitate Dei CSEL 40

conf. = *Confessions*
WSA I.1
Confessiones Bibliothèque Augustinienne 13–14 (Paris: Études Augustinennes, 1962)

dial. = *On Dialectic*
De dialectica. B.D. Jackson *De dialectica* Synthese Historical Library 16.
 Dordrecht: Reidel, 1975

doc. Chr. = *On Christian Doctrine*
D.W. Robertson *Augustine: On Christian Doctrine* Library of Liberal Arts
 80 (Indianapolis: Bobbs-Merrill, 1958)
De doctrina Christiana CCL 32

en.Ps. = Expositions of the Psalms
WSA III.14–17
Enarrationes in Psalmos CCL 38– 40

ep. = *Epistles*
WSA II.1–3
Epistulae PL 33

ep.Jo. = *Homilies on the First Epistle of John*
WSA III.13; FC 92
In epistulam Joannis ad Parthos tractatus SC 75

c. Faust. = Against Faustus
NPNF 4
Contra Faustum CSEL 25.1

Gn.litt. = *Literal Commentary on Genesis*
WSA I.13; ACW 41–42
De Genesi ad litteram CSEL 28.1

Gn.litt.imp. = On the Literal Interpretation of Genesis, an Unfinished Book
FC 84
De Genesi ad litteram imperfectus liber CSEL 28.1

Jo.eu.tr. = *Tractates on the Gospel of John*
WSA III.12; FC 78, 79, 88, 90, 92
In Johaniis euangelium tractatus CCL 36

mag. = The Teacher
WSA 1.3
De Magistro CCL 29

mus. = *On Music*
Books 1–5 – FC 4
Book 6 – Martin Jacobsson. 2002. *De musica liber VI* (critical edition
 with a translation and introduction) Studia Latina Stockholmiensia
 XLVII. Stockholm, Sweden: Almqvist & Wiksell
De musica CSEL 102

ord. = *On Order*
FC 5 *Divine Providence and the Problem of Evil*
De ordine CCL 29

op. mon. = *On the Work of Monks*
FC 16
De opere monachorum CSEL 41

quant. = *On the Greatness of the Soul*
FC 4
De animae quantitate CSEL 89

retr. = Retractations
FC 60
Retractationes CSEL 36

s. = *Sermons*
WSA III.1–11
Sermones CCL 41

Simpl. = To Simplicianus
LCC 6
Ad Simplicianum CCL 44

sol. = *Soliloquies*
FC 2
Soliloquia CSEL 89

trin. = The Trinity
WSA I.5
De trinitate CCL 50/50A

uera.rel. = On True Religion
LCC 6
De uera religione CSEL 77

Gregory of Nyssa

Inscriptions on the Psalms

Ronald E. Heine, *Gregory of Nyssa's Treastise on the Inscriptions of the Psalms* (Oxford: Oxford University Press, 1995)
In inscriptiones Psalmorum Gregorii Nysseni Opera V (Leiden, Brill)

Nicetas of Remesiana

Liturgical Singing

FC 7, 65–76

De utilitate hymnorum – C.H. Turner text of *De uigiliis* and *De utilitate hymnorum* based on Cod. Vatic.Reg. lat. 131, saec 3–10 in *Journal of Theological Studies* 22, 24.

Secondary Literature

Abert, Hermann. 1964. *Die Musikanschauung Des Mittelalters Und Ihre Grundlagen.* Harvard, MS: Harvard University Press.

Alexander, Gavin. 2001. 'Sidney's Interruptions'. *Studies in Philology* 98 (2): 184–204.

Allberry, C.R.C. 1938. *A Manichaean Psalm Book.* Stuttgart: Kohlhammer.

Anderson, David (trans.) 1980. *On the Holy Spirit.* New York, NY: St Vladimir's Seminary Press.

Andreopoulos, Andreas, Augustine Casiday, and Carol Harrison (eds.) 2011. *Meditations of the Heart: The Psalms in Early Christian Thought and Practice: Essays in Honour of Andrew Louth.* Studia Traditionis Theologiae 8. Turnhout: Brepols.

Arnold, D.W.H, and Pamela Bright (eds.) 1995. *De Doctrina Christiana. A Classic of Western Culture.* Indiana: Notre Dame.

Ayres, Lewis. 2010. *Augustine and the Trinity.* Cambridge: Cambridge University Press.

Ayres, Lewis, and Gareth Jones. 1998. *Christian Origins: Theology, Rhetoric and Community.* 1 edition. London; New York: Routledge.

Balthasar, Hans Urs von. 1984. *The Glory of the Lord: A Theological Aesthetics*, volume 2. Edinburgh: T&T Clark.

Barker, Andrew. 1984. *Greek Musical Writings.* Cambridge Readings in the Literature of Music. Cambridge: Cambridge University Press.

Barnes, Julian. 2013. *Levels of Life.* London: Jonathan Cape.

Barthes, Roland. 1977. *Image, Music, Text.* London: Fontana.

Begbie, Jeremy, and Steven R. Guthrie. 2011. *Resonant Witness: Conversations between Music and Theology.* Calvin Institute of Christian Worship. Liturgical Studies Series Grand Rapids, MI: Eerdmans.

Bettetini, M. 1991. 'Stato della questione e bibliografia ragionata sul dialogo De Musica di Sant'Agostino (1940–90)'. *Rivista di filosofia neo-scolastica* 83: 430–469.

Beyenka, M. Melchior. 1957. 'St. Augustine and the Hymns of St. Ambrose'. *American Benedictine Review* 8 (2):121.

Biffi, Inos. 2003. *Fede, Poesia e Canto Del Mistero Di Cristo in Ambrogio, Agostino e Paolino Di Aquileia*. Biblioteca Di Cultura Medievale. Milan: Jaca.

Bitton-Ashkelony, Bruria, Theodore De Bruyn, and Carol Harrison. 2015. *Patristic Studies in the Twenty-First Century: Proceedings of an International Conference to Mark the 50th Anniversary of the International Association of Patristic Studies*. Turnhout, Belgium: Brepols.

Blacking, John. 1994. *John Blacking: Dialogue with the Ancestors*. John Blacking Memorial Lecture, 1991. London: Goldsmith's College.

Blackwood, Stephen. 2015. *The Consolation of Boethius as Poetic Liturgy*. Oxford Early Christian Studies. Oxford: Oxford University Press.

Boyle, Marjorie O'Rourke. 2007. 'Augustine's Heartbeat: From Time to Eternity'. *Viator – Medieval and Renaissance Studies* 38 (1): 19–43.

Brachtendorf, J. 1997. 'Cicero and Augustine on the Passions'. *Revue d'Études Augustiniennes et Patristiques* 43 (2): 289–308.

Braund, Susanna Morton, and Christopher Gill (eds.) 1997. *The Passions in Roman Thought and Literature*. Cambridge, UK; New York, NY: Cambridge University Press.

Brennan, Brian. 1988. 'Augustine's "De Musica"'. *Vigiliae Christianae* 42 (3): 267–281.

Burns, Paul. 1993. 'Augustine's Distinctive Use of the Psalms in the Confessions: The Role of Music and Recitation'. *Augustinian Studies* 24: 133.

Burton, Philip. 2007. *Language in the Confessions of Augustine*. Oxford: Oxford University Press.

Butler, Shane. 2015. *The Ancient Phonograph*. New York: Zone.

Byers, Sarah Catherine. 2013. *Perception, Sensibility, and Moral Motivation in Augustine: A Stoic-Platonic Synthesis*. Cambridge: Cambridge University Press.

Cameron, Michael. 2012. *Christ Meets Me Everywhere: Augustine's Early Figurative Exegesis*. Oxford Studies in Historical Theology. Oxford: Oxford University Press.

Carruthers, M. 1990. *A Book of Memory: A Study of Memory in Medieval Culture*. Cambridge: Cambridge University Press.

Caston, Ruth Rothaus, and Robert A. Kaster. 2016. *Hope, Joy, and Affection in the Classical World*. Emotions of the Past. New York, NY: Oxford University Press.

Chambers, C.B. 1973. *Folksong – Plainsong: A Study in Origins and Musical Relationships*. London: Merlin.

Charlet, Jean-Louis. 1985. 'L'inspiration et la form bibliques dans la poésie latine, du IIIe au Vie siècle' in Fontaine and Pietri (eds.) 1985: 613–644.

Charru, Philippe. 2009. 'Temps et Musique dans La Pensée d'Augustin'. *Revue d'Études Augustiniennes et Patristiques* 55 (2): 171–188.

Clark, Gillian. 2015. *Monica. An Ordinary Saint*. Oxford: Oxford University Press.

Clark, Gillian. 2016. '*Caritas:* Augustine on Love and Fellow Feeling' in Caston and Kaster (eds.) 2016: 209–225.

Clark, Gillian. 2017. 'In Praise of the Wax Candle: Augustine the Poet and Late Latin Literature' in Elsner, Jas and Jesús Hernández Lobato (eds.) *The Poetics of Late Latin Literature*. Oxford: Oxford University Press.

Colish, Marcia L. 1968. *The Mirror of Language: A Study in the Medieval Theory of Knowledge*. Yale: Yale University Press.

Colish, Marcia L. 1985. *The Stoic Tradition from Antiquity to the Early Middle Ages*. Studies in the History of Christian Thought. Leiden: E.J. Brill.

Conybeare, Catherine. 2006. *The Irrational Augustine*. Oxford: Oxford University Press.

Conybeare, Catherine. 2012. 'Reading the Confessions' in Vessey (ed.) 2012: 99–112.

Conybeare, Catherine. 2012a. 'Beyond Word and Image: Aural Patterning in Augustine's Confessions' in De Nie and Noble (eds.) 2012: 143–164.

Copeland, Rita, and I. Sluiter. 2009. *Medieval Grammar and Rhetoric: Language Arts and Literary Theory, AD 300–1475*. Oxford: Oxford University Press.

Court, Raymond. 1987. *Sagesse de l'art: Arts Plastiques, Musique, Philosophie*. Paris: Méridiens Klincksieck.

Cunningham, Maurice. 1955. 'The Place of the Hymns of St. Ambrose in the Latin Poetic Tradition'. *Studies in Philology* 52: 509.

Davenson, Henri. 1942. *Traité de La Musique Selon l'esprit de Saint Augustin*. Les Cahiers du Rhône. Neuchatel: La Baconnière; Paris: Éditions du Seuil.

Deproost, Paul-Augustin. 2010. '"Au Commencement" Entre Mémoire et Désir, La Réponse Augustinienne à l'énigme Du Temps'. *Revue Théologique de Louvain* 41–3: 313–344.

Du Roy, Olivier. 1966. *L'intelligence de la foi en la Trinité selon saint Augustin: genèse de sa théologie trinitaire jusqu'en 391*. Paris: Études Augustiniennes.

Dudden, F. Homes. 1935. *The Life and Times of St. Ambrose*. Oxford: Clarendon Press.

Dunkle, Brian. 2016. *Enchantment and Creed in the Hymns of Ambrose of Milan*. Oxford Early Christian Studies. Oxford: Oxford University Press.

Dusen, David Van. 2014. *The Space of Time: A Sensualist Interpretation of Time in Augustine, Confessions X to XII*. Leiden: Brill.

Esler, Philip Francis (ed.) 2000. *The Early Christian World*. London: Routledge.

Fagles, Robert (trans.) 1996. *Homer the Odyssey*. Bath: The Softback Preview.

Fagles, Robert (trans.) 1997. *Homer the Iliad*. Bath: The Softback Preview.

Fiedrowicz, Michael. 1997. *Psalmus vox totius Christi: Studien zu Augustins 'Enarrationes in Psalmos'*. Freiburg: Herder.

Fitzgerald, John T. 2008. *Passions and Moral Progress in Greco-Roman Thought*. London; New York: Routledge.

Fontaine, Jacques (ed.) 1992. *Hymnes. Ambroise de Milan; texte établi, traduit et annoté*. Paris: Cerf.

Fontaine, Jacques, and Charles Pietri. 1985. *Le Monde latin antique et la Bible*. Bible de tous les temps vol. 2. Paris: Beauchesne.

Frank, Georgia. 2000. *The Memory of the Eyes: Pilgrims to Living Saints in Christian Late Antiquity*. Transformation of the Classical Heritage 30. Berkeley; London: University of California Press.

Gerber, Chad Tyler. 2012. *The Spirit of Augustine's Early Theology: Contextualizing Augustine's Pneumatology*. Ashgate: Farnham.

Gioia, Luigi. 2008. *The Theological Epistemology of Augustine's De Trinitate*. Oxford Theological Monographs. Oxford: Oxford University Press.

Gordley, Matthew E. 2011. *Teaching through Song in Antiquity: Didactic Hymnody among Greeks, Romans, Jews, and Christians*. Wissenschaftliche Untersuchungen Zum Neuen Testament 2. Reihe 302. Tübingen: Mohr Siebeck.

Graver, Margaret. 2007. *Stoicism and Emotion*. Chicago, IL; London: University of Chicago Press.

Gross, Daniel M. 2006. *The Secret History of Emotion: From Aristotle's Rhetoric to Modern Brain Science*. Chicago, IL; London: University of Chicago Press.

Habinek, Thomas N. 2005. *The World of Roman Song: From Ritualized Speech to Social Order*. Baltimore; London: Johns Hopkins University Press.

Hadot, Ilsetraut. 1984. *Artes Libéraux et philosophie dans la pensée antique*. Paris: Études Augustiniennes.

Hadot, Pierre. 1998. *The Inner Citadel: The Meditations of Marcus Aurelius*. Cambridge, MA; London: Harvard University Press.

Hamburger, Jeffrey F., and Anne-Marie Bouché (eds.) 2006. *The Mind's Eye: Art and Theological Argument in the Middle Ages*. Princeton, NJ: Department of Art and Archaeology, Princeton University in association with Princeton University Press.

Hammond, C.J.-B. 2012. 'A Love Supreme: Augustine's "Jazz" of Theology'. *Augustinian Studies* 43 (1–2): 149–177.

Hammond, C.J.-B. 2014. *Augustine. Confessions.* 2 vols. Loeb, 26–27.

Harmless, William. 1995. *Augustine and the Catechumenate.* Collegeville, MN: Liturgical Press.

Harmless, William. 2008. *Mystics.* Oxford: Oxford University Press.

Harrison, Carol. 1992. *Beauty and Revelation in the Thought of Saint Augustine.* Oxford Theological Monographs. Oxford: Clarendon Press.

Harrison, Carol. 2006. *Rethinking Augustine's Early Theology: An Argument for Continuity.* Oxford: Oxford University Press.

Harrison, Carol. 2010. 'Transformative Listening: Constructing the Hearer in Early Christianity' in *Studia Patristica.* Leuven: Peeters, 427–432.

Harrison, Carol. 2011. 'Enchanting the Soul: The Music of the Psalms' in Andreopoulos, Casiday and Harrison (eds.) 205–223.

Harrison, Carol. 2013. *The Art of Listening in the Early Church.* Oxford: Oxford University Press.

Harrison, Carol. 2015. 'Getting Carried Away: Why Did Augustine Sing?' *Augustinian Studies* 46 (1): 1–22.

Harvey, Susan Ashbrook. 2006. *Scenting Salvation: Ancient Christianity and the Olfactory Imagination.* Transformation of the Classical Heritage 42. Berkeley, CA: University of California.

Harvey, Susan Ashbrook. 2015. 'Patristic Worlds' in Ashkelony, B. Bitton, T. De Bruyn, and C. Harrison (eds.) 2015: 25–56.

Heine, R.E. 1997. *Gregory of Nyssa Treatise on the Inscriptions of the Psalms* Oxford Early Christian Texts. Oxford: Oxford University Press.

Heninger, S.K. 1974. *Touches of Sweet Harmony: Pythagorean Cosmology and Renaissance Poetics.* San Marino, CA: Huntington Library.

Hentschel, F. 2002. De Musica. Bücher I und VI: vom ästhetischen Urteil zur metaphysischen Erkenntnis. Hamburg: Felix Meiner.

Hentschel, Frank. 2011. 'The Sensuous Music Aesthetics of the Middle Ages: The Cases of Augustine, Jacques de Liège and Guido of Arezzo'. *Plainsong and Medieval Music* 20 (1): 1–29.

Hermanowicz, Erika T. 2004. 'Book Six of Augustine's De musica and the Episcopal Embassies of 408'. *Augustinian Studies* 35: 165–198.

Homer. 1998. *The Iliad.* London: Penguin.

Huré, Jean. 1924. *Saint Augustin Musicien. D'après Le 'De Musica' et Différentes Pages de Ses Oeuvres Consacrées à La Musique.* Paris: De Boccard.

Jeserich, Philipp. 2013. *Musica Naturalis: Speculative Music Theory and Poetics, from Saint Augustine to the Late Middle Ages in France.* Rethinking Theory. Baltimore, MD: Johns Hopkins University Press.

Kaster, Robert A. 1988. *Guardians of Language: The Grammarian and Society in Late Antiquity*. Transformation of the Classical Heritage 11. Berkeley: University of California Press.

Kaster, Robert A. 2005. *Emotion, Restraint, and Community in Ancient Rome*. Classical Culture and Society. New York; Oxford: Oxford University Press.

Katô, Takeshi. 1966. 'Melodia Interior. Sur Le Traité De Pulchro et Apto'. *Revue d'Etudes Augustiniennes et Patristiques* 12 (3–4): 229–240.

King, J. Christopher. 2005. *Origen on the Song of Songs as the Spirit of Scripture: The Bridegroom's Perfect Marriage-Song*. Oxford: Oxford University Press.

Knauer, Georg Nicolaus. 1955. *Psalmenzitate in Augustins Konfessionen*. Göttingen: Vandenhoeck & Ruprecht.

Kolbet, Paul R. 2006. 'Athanasius, the Psalms, and the Reformation of the Self'. *Harvard Theological Review* 99 (1): 85–101.

Kotzé, Annemare. 2001. 'Reading Psalm 4 to the Manicheans'. *Vigiliae Christianae* 55 (2): 119–136.

La Croix, Richard R. 1988. *Augustine on Music: An Interdisciplinary Collection of Essays*. Studies in the History and Interpretation of Music 6. Lewiston; Lampeter: Edwin Mellen Press.

Lagorio, Valerie Marie, and Anne Clark Bartlett (eds.) 1995. *Vox Mystica: Essays on Medieval Mysticism in Honor of Professor Valerie M. Lagorio*. Cambridge; Rochester, NY: Brewer.

Lambot, C. (ed.) 1935. 'Texte completé et amendé du Psalmus contra partem Donati de Saint Augustin'. *Revue Bénédictine*: 312–330.

Lattke, Michael. 1979. *Die Oden Salomos in ihrer Bedeutung für Neues Testament und Gnosis*. Orbis biblicus et orientalis 25. Fribourg; Göttingen: Vandenhoeck & Ruprecht.

Lattke, Michael. 1991. *Hymnus: Materialien zu einer Geschichte der antiken Hymnologie*. Novum Testamentum et orbis antiquus; 19. Freiburg; Göttingen: Vandenhoeck & Ruprecht.

Lories, Danielle, and L. Rizzerio. 2003. *De la phantasia à l'imagination*. Louvain: Peeters.

MacCormack, Sabine. 1998. *The Shadows of Poetry: Vergil in the Mind of Augustine*. Transformation of the Classical Heritage 26. Berkeley; London: University of California Press.

Markus, R.A. 1995. 'Signs, Communication and Communities in Augustine's *De doctrina christiana*' in Arnold, D.W.H and Pamela Bright (eds.) 1995: 97–108.

Marrou, Henri Irénée. 1958. *Saint Augustin et la fin de la culture antique*. Paris: Boccard.

Mathiesen, Thomas J. 1999. *Apollo's Lyre: Greek Music and Music Theory in Antiquity and the Middle Ages*. Lincoln, Nebraska; London: University of Nebraska Press.

McGilchrist, Iain. 2010. *The Master and His Emissary: The Divided Brain and the Making of the Western World*. New Haven: Yale University Press.

McKinnon, James. 1987. *Music in Early Christian Literature*. Cambridge Readings in the Literature of Music. Cambridge: Cambridge University Press.

McKinnon, James. 1996. 'Preface to the Study of the Alleluia'. *Early Music History* 15: 213.

McKinnon, James. 2000. 'Music' in Esler 773–790.

McLynn, Neil B. 1994. *Ambrose of Milan: Church and Court in a Christian Capital*. Transformation of the Classical Heritage 22. Berkeley; London: University of California Press.

Miller, Patricia Cox. 1994. *Dreams in Late Antiquity: Studies in the Imagination of a Culture*. Princeton, NJ: Princeton University Press.

Miller, Patricia Cox. 2009. *The Corporeal Imagination: Signifying the Holy in Late Ancient Christianity*. Pennsylvania: University of Pennsylvania Press.

Mithen, Steven J. 2005. *The Singing Neanderthals: The Origins of Music, Language, Mind and Body*. London: Weidenfeld & Nicolson.

Moorhead, John. 2010. 'Ambrose and Augustine on Hymns'. *Downside Review* 128: 79–92.

Mountford, J.F. 1964. 'Music and the Romans'. *Bulletin of the John Rylands Library* 47: 198–211.

Murphy, Joseph. 1979. 'The "Contra Hilarum" of Augustine, Its Liturgical and Musical Implications'. *Augustinian Studies* 10: 133.

Natoli, Bartolo. 2008. 'The Liminal Hymn: Deus Creator Omnium in Augustine's Confessions'. Unpublished paper.

Nie, Giselle de, and Thomas F.X. Noble. 2012. *Envisioning Experience in Late Antiquity and the Middle Ages: Dynamic Patterns in Texts and Images*. Farnham: Ashgate.

Nussbaum, Martha Craven. 1994. *The Therapy of Desire: Theory and Practice in Hellenistic Ethics*. Princeton: Princeton University Press.

Nussbaum, Martha Craven. 2003. *Upheavals of Thought: The Intelligence of Emotions*. Cambridge: Cambridge University Press.

O'Connell, Robert J. 1978. *Art and the Christian Intelligence in St. Augustine*. Oxford: Blackwell.

O'Donnell, J.J. 1992. *Augustine: Confessions (Introduction, Text and Commentary)*. 3 vols. Oxford: Clarendon Press.

Page, Christopher. 2010. *The Christian West and Its Singers: The First Thousand Years*. New Haven: Yale University Press.

Perl, Carl Johann, and Alan Kriegsman. 1955. 'Augustine and Music: On the Occasion of the 1600th Anniversary of the Saint'. *The Musical Quarterly* 41 (4): 496–510.

Petersen, Nils H. 2012. 'St. Augustine in Twentieth-Century Music'. 2012.

Pickstock, Catherine. 1998. 'The Musical Imperative'. *Angelaki* 3 (2): 7–29.

Pickstock, Catherine. 1999. 'Music: Soul, City and Cosmos after Augustine' in Milbank, John, Catherine Pickstock, and Graham Ward (eds.) *Radical Orthodoxy*. London: Routledge, 243–277.

Pinborg, Jan, and B. Darrell Jackson. 1975. *Augustine De Dialectica*. New York, NY: Springer.

Polanyi, Michael. 1958. *Personal Knowledge: Towards a Post-Critical Philosophy*. London: Routledge & Kegan Paul.

Potter, John. 2012. *A History of Singing*. Cambridge: Cambridge University Press.

Potter, John, and Neil Sorrell. 2012. *A History of Singing*. Cambridge: Cambridge University Press.

Puech, Henri-Charles. 1968. 'Musique et hymnologie Manicheennes'. *Encylclopedie des musiques sacrées* 1: 354–386.

Quasten, Johannes. 1988. *Music and Worship in Pagan and Christian Antiquity*. Translated by Ramsay, Boniface. Washington, DC: Pastoral Press.

Ramsey, Boniface. 1997. *Ambrose*. Early Church Fathers. London: Routledge.

Rist, John M. 1994. *Augustine: Ancient Thought Baptized*. Cambridge: Cambridge University Press.

Roche, W. 1941. 'Measure, Number and Weight in Saint Augustine'. *New Scholasticism* 15: 350–376.

Russell, D.A., and M. Winterbottom (ed.) 1972. *Ancient Literary Criticism*. Oxford: Clarendon Press, 472.

Scully, Ellen R. 2013. 'De Musica as the Guide to Understanding Augustine's Trinitarian Numerology in the De Trinitate'. *Augustinian Studies* 44 (1): 93–116.

Sheerin, Daniel. 1982. '"Celeuma" in Christian Latin: Lexical and Literary Notes'. *Traditio* 38: 45.

Shirt, David John. 2015. *'Sing to the Lord with the Harp': Attitudes to Musical Instruments in Early Christianity, 680*. Doctoral thesis, Durham University.

Sieben, H.J. 1977. 'Der Psalter und die Bekehrung der VOCES und AFFECTUS. Zu Augustinus, Conf. IX,4,6 und X,33'. *Theologie und Philosophie* 52: 481–497.

Simonetti, Manlio. 1952. *Studi sull'innologia popolare cristiana dei primi secoli*. Atti della Accademia nazionale dei Lincei. Roma: Accademia Nazionale dei Lincei.

Solignac, A. 1958. 'Doxographies et Manuels dans la formation de saint Augustin'. *Revue des Études Augustiniennes* 1. 113–148.

Solignac, Aimé. 1983. 'Passions et vie spirituelle' in *Dictionnaire de Spiritualité*. 339–357.

Smith, John Arthur. 2011. *Music in Ancient Judaism and Early Christianity*. Farnham: Ashgate.

Sorabji, Richard. 2000. *Emotion and Peace of Mind: From Stoic Agitation to Christian Temptation*. Gifford Lectures. Oxford: Oxford University Press.

Stapert, Calvin. 2007. *A New Song for an Old World: Musical Thought in the Early Church*. Calvin Institute of Christian Worship Liturgical Studies Series. Grand Rapids, MI; Cambridge: Eerdmans.

Stoltzfus, Philip Edward. 2006. *Theology as Performance: Music, Aesthetics, and God in Western Thought*. New York; London: T&T Clark.

Stone-Davis, Férdia J. 2011. *Musical Beauty: Negotiating the Boundary between Subject and Object*. Eugene, OR: Wipf and Stock Cascade Books.

Stone-Davis, Férdia J. 'The Harmony of the Spheres: Sound, Silence and the Expression of the Unknowable'. BIRTHA Medieval Postgraduate Conference 2010: Language and Silence (26–27 February).

Svoboda, Karel. 1933. *L'esthétique de saint Augustin et ses sources*. Brno: Vydàvà filosofickà fakulta.

Thonnard, F.J. 1953. 'La vie affective de l'âme selon s. Augustin'. *Année Théologique Augustinienne* 14–15: 33–53.

Treitler, Leo. 2003. *With Voice and Pen: Coming to Know Medieval Song and How It Was Made*. Oxford: Oxford University Press.

Van der Meer, F. 1961. *Augustine the Bishop*. London and New York: Sheed and Ward.

Verheul, Ambroise. 1983. 'La Spiritualité Du Chant Liturgique Chez Saint Paul et Saint Augustin'. 1983.

Vessey, Mark. 2012. *A Companion to Augustine*. Chichester, West Sussex; Malden, MA: John Wiley.

Vroom, H. 1933. *Le Psaume Abécédaire de Saint Augustin et La Poésie Latine Rythmique*. Nijmegen: Dekker.

Vuolanto, Dr Ville. 2015. *Children and Asceticism in Late Antiquity: Continuity, Family Dynamics and the Rise of Christianity*. London: Ashgate.

Walhout, Clarence. 1979. 'On Symbolic Meanings: Augustine and Ricoeur'. *Renascence* 31 (2): 115–127.

Werner, Eric. 1959. *The Sacred Bridge: The Interdependence of Liturgy and Music in Synagogue and Church during the First Millennium*. London: New York: Dennis Dobson; Columbia University Press.

Westermeyer, Paul. 1998. *Te Deum: Church and Music*. Minneapolis, MN: Augsberg Fortress.

White, Carolinne. 2000. *Early Christian Latin Poets*. Early Church Fathers. London: Routledge.

Wille, Günther. 1967. *Musica Romana: die Bedeutung der Musik im Leben der Römer*. Amsterdam: PSchippers.

Williams, A.N. 2007. *The Divine Sense: The Intellect in Patristic Theology*. Cambridge: Cambridge University Press.

Williams, Michael Stuart. 2013. 'Hymns as Acclamations: The Case of Ambrose of Milan'. *Journal of Late Antiquity* 6 (1): 108–134.

Wulf, Silke. 2013. *Zeit der Musik: Vom Hören der Warheit in Augustinus' De Musica*. Fribourg: Karl Alber.

Zahl, Simeon. 2015. 'On the Affective Salience of Doctrines'. *Modern Theology* 31 (3): 428.

Zorzi, M. Benedetta. 2002. 'Melos e iubilus nelle Enarrationes in Psalmos di Agostino: Una questione di mistica agostiniana'. *Augustinianum* 42 (2): 383–413.

INDEX